D1188520

THE

CRIES
OF MY

The Resiliency of the Human Spirit

RODRIGO T. GABRIEL

WESTBOW
PRESS®
A DIVISION OF THOMAS NELSON
& ZONDERVAN

WestBow Press books may be ordered through booksellers or by contacting:

WestBow Press
A Division of Thomas Nelson & Zondervan
1663 Liberty Drive
Bloomington, IN 47403
www.westbowpress.com
844-714-3454

ISBN: 978-1-6642-1043-1 (sc)
ISBN: 978-1-6642-1042-4 (hc)
ISBN: 978-1-6642-1044-8 (e)

Library of Congress Control Number: 2020921121

Print information available on the last page.

WestBow Press rev. date: 11/24/2020

CONTENTS

ACKNOWLEDGMENTS

With profound gratitude, I acknowledge the immense love and support of my wonderful wife, Sylvia, as well as that of my eldest daughter, Bernadette, who endured with me years of enormous hardships and sacrifices, particularly during Melissa's critical chemotherapy treatment. Special thanks also to both of our parents, siblings and to all of our relatives in the United States and in the Philippines, who extended different forms of assistance. Their constant prayers were very much appreciated.

My special appreciation to Sylvia's mother, Mrs. Rosario Tiña, who agreed to come to the United States to help us, which was a true testament of her love and concern for us. Her stay lasted for a year. She also had her own share of sacrifices, being away from her husband in the Philippines during that same period. Her tireless efforts in handling the daily household chores certainly lightened our burden. Her presence alone provided us with another shoulder to cry on as well as vitally needed emotional support.

Much gratitude to all the medical staff at the Children's Hospital of New Jersey, particularly Dr. Walters, Dr. Ryan, and Dr. Nepo; the head nurse, Ms. Alice Rennick; and the other attending nurses, all of whom worked very hard and genuinely tried their best to make Melissa's condition a bit more bearable while at the hospital.

Similarly, I would like to thank some of my coworkers for their support, especially Walter Mullins, whose kind and generous offer to help me and my family in any way possible was quite touching.

I very much appreciated the amazing kindness of Ms. Lynch, Melissa's first- grade teacher at Emma Arleth Elementary School in Parlin, New Jersey, who volunteered to home-tutor Melissa for about four years.

Much appreciation also to all of Melissa's teachers, who wrote a heartwarming poem dedicated for her; as well as to all of her classmates, who collectively created and personally signed an endearing huge card of sympathy.

Many thanks also for the incredible support of the volunteer drivers at the American Cancer Society and to the staff at the Starlight Foundation for granting Melissa's last wish for a weeklong religious trip to Lourdes, France.

Finally, my deepest acknowledgment to my immediate family, who are the dearest and nearest to my heart: my wife, Sylvia; my daughter Bernadette; and my son, Bobby, all of whom served wholeheartedly as my editorial board.

INTRODUCTION

The Cries of My Soul is a portrayal of my life experiences, both as a child and as an adult. It describes in great detail my childhood years and humble beginnings. It was in a small barrio named Makinabang, in the township of Baliwag, where I was born, a poor rural area north of Manila, the capital city of the Philippines. My hometown's population during the mid-1940s was roughly three thousand, and the main livelihood was agricultural farming, predominantly rice and corn.

The focal point of *The Cries of My Soul*, however, is the extraordinary life of my second daughter, Melissa, who was born in the United States on May 27, 1976. She was truly special, remarkably kind, and a very loving young girl whose inspiring life was cut short by a malignant blood disorder disease known as acute lymphocytic leukemia. She was only twelve years old when she lost her battle, passing away on October 9, 1988.

The Cries of My Soul is a true chronicle of the events of Melissa's inspirational life, based largely on her own diary with some select entries woven throughout the chapters. Also highlighted are her poignant poems and heartbreaking last writings.

A few weeks after returning from a religious trip to Lourdes, France, in late September of 1988, her last wish, Melissa reflected on her spiritual experience in Lourdes, which gave her a feeling that her life here on earth had just been fulfilled. Consequently, she gallantly expressed her readiness and willingness to rejoin her Creator.

Having personally witnessed the incredible courage and the righteous way in which Melissa lived her short life undoubtedly changed my perspective on life in significant ways. It took me more than thirty years to finally gain the courage and strength to authentically write this book about my family's staggering journey through life's overwhelming challenges.

What cannot be underestimated, however, is the resiliency of the human spirit that is anchored by a deep faith in the almighty God.

BACKGROUND

Following are some of the historical events that happened during 1945, the year of my birth:

- March 9–10, 1945—The deadliest air raid of the Pacific war claimed the lives of eighty thousand to one hundred thousand Japanese civilians when the US attacked Tokyo with incendiary bombs.
- February–May 1945—The surrender of Nazi Germany.
- August 6, 1945—The American B-29 bomber dropped the first atomic bomb in Hiroshima, which killed ninety thousand to one hundred forty-six thousand Japanese, some of whom would later die of radiation exposure.
- August 9, 1945—The second atomic bomb was dropped in Nagasaki, claiming the lives of thirty-nine thousand to eighty thousand. Roughly half the deaths in each city occurred on the first day.
- September 2, 1945—The surrender of Imperial Japan was formally signed, bringing the hostilities of World War II to a close.
- October 24, 1945—The founding of the United Nations.

Such archival events served as a backdrop to the year when I first saw light. It was a year of overwhelming conflict and unparalleled devastation, but also a year that saw the promise of an enduring peace.

CHAPTER 1

Early Childhood Years

BEING RAISED IN absolute poverty, I saw, up close and personal, the daily struggles of my family, and we weathered life's tremendous hardships together. We lacked even basic necessities such as running water and electricity. On several occasions, we even experienced the harsh reality of not having enough food to eat.

However, at the dinner table, my parents would always convey a positive message, encouraging us to have an attitude of gratitude even for the very limited things we had and for being together as a happy family. They instilled in us the importance of perseverance, the value of hard work and resiliency, and the idea that life's difficulties should not defeat us. They taught us to strive for a better future and to do the right thing no matter what.

My family's unfortunate financial difficulties during the early years was exacerbated by the fact that we were a large family with eight children, all from a father who had no permanent job and a mother who was a housewife. This predicament tested my resiliency at an early age and prepared me to adapt to any situation.

Since all our neighbors were in the same dilemma, it seemed to me that such a way of life was normal and that the everyday struggles, at least on the surface, were never really felt by everybody. The cycle of poverty was prevalent in my neighborhood. Most children, like their parents, married young and had many children of their own with very little or no education. To most neighborhood children, it seemed as though the grip of poverty was inescapable.

Despite all the hardships, my parents instilled in us the importance of prayer and faith. They prayed every day before going to bed and very early in the morning before breakfast time. At several of these early-morning prayer gatherings as a child, I would fall asleep and my father would gently tap the back of my head to wake me up.

Even at an early age, seeing my mother cry in family prayer gatherings left a scar on my heart. My mother served as the leader of a prayer group. As part of their commitment, they performed night prayer services whenever a community member passed away.

As part of the traditional religious rituals during the Lenten season, my parents would read aloud biblical passages pertaining to the life and times of Jesus Christ in a certain rhythmic way, which sounded like a mixture of a poem and a classical song.

Our house where I was born was akin to a larger version of a nipa hut, with stairs and floors made of bamboo. The roof was made of nipa palm stitched together by very fine bamboo strings, and the windows had wooden frames with several small square seashells encased in the middle section. The first floor was plain dirt. We kept some chickens inside a bamboo cage and two dogs in another cage on the floor.

The kitchen window was made of nipa palm, and we used a piece of bamboo to push it wide open. Our stove was made of clay with the middle part deep enough to hold firewood with three equally sized round pieces of overhang clay at the top to serve as pot holders. This early cooking practice was primitive compared to the modern way of cooking using natural gas and electricity.

Of course we did not have the modern conveniences such as a refrigerator, a television, a telephone, beds with mattresses, a bathroom with a toilet and shower, a living room set, a microwave, an oven, or a car. We had a small transistor radio, which was our sole source of news and entertainment. There was a bed made of rattan in the only bedroom, occupied by my parents. We children slept on a handwoven mat on the bamboo floor with mosquito nets. Our blanket was made of discarded small pieces of cloth in varying colors and was hand-stitched together by my mother. After a while, the blanket became super heavy as my mother added more cloth to it.

My mother kept some food in a large basket that hung from a metal hook anchored to a bamboo plank in the middle of the kitchen ceiling. She did this to keep the food out of reach of the cats.

One afternoon I came home from school very hungry. I decided to get the food myself, using a chair. I could barely reach the bottom of the basket, and I did not realize that the basket was pretty heavy with lots of leftover food, including a big bowl of lentil soup. While I was trying to push the basket up to get it off the hook, the basket tilted to one side and the soup started to drip down my right hand and down the right side of my body. I laughed at first, but then I started to cry as I knew my mother would reprimand me for not asking her for assistance.

One afternoon as a very young boy, I was sitting on the middle step of the stairs looking down at the dogs and the chickens. Suddenly I became very dizzy and felt like things were swirling around. I was about to fall down the stairs. Fortunately, my mother saw me. She grabbed me by my chest and took me upstairs. She felt my forehead, which was very warm, an indication that my fever was high. Because of our impoverished condition, consulting a doctor was never an option, and we did not have a thermometer to accurately gauge the fever level. My mother told me to lie down. After I did so, she put a wet towel on my forehead. It smelled like it was soaked in vinegar. My mother explained later on that this practice was used in the early days to help alleviate a fever. I was also given an orange soda in lieu of medicine. It was only when we were sick that we were able to have soda.

Since the window was open at the time, a butterfly had flown inside the house. In the early days, there was a superstitious belief that it was a bad omen for a butterfly to be inside the house when somebody was sick.

My mother started to cry and was praying ardently, saying, "Please, God, help my son. Please don't take him away. He is just too young to die." After a few hours, my condition improved. I gradually felt better.

When I was about eight years old, I vividly remember being accompanied by my mother to the rice field during rice harvest season.

We never owned a rice field; her goal was to gather some of the leftover rice grains that had spilled from the threshing machine. Since the temperature in the Philippines during the summertime averaged around ninety-five degrees Fahrenheit, my mother would usually wear a very large native hat made of nipa palm covered by a light-colored bandanna.

She would also bring the circular basket that she used to separate the rice grains from the dirt. She would gather small amounts of the rice grains covered in dirt and put them inside the circular basket. She would then slowly tip the basket, holding the top and the bottom, so that the rice grains and the dirt would roll down toward the ground. Since the dirt was heavier than the rice grains, the dirt normally rolled straight down, while the rice grains, with help from the wind, would roll down a few inches away from where the dirt had landed and then roll into the handwoven mat my mother had strategically positioned on the ground. The process was tedious. In order to gather a significant amount of clean rice, she would do this maybe a hundred times.

Because of the unforgiving heat from the burning sun, she would occasionally wipe away her sweat, mixed with tears, running down her cheeks.

Once I asked her why she was crying, and she responded, "Son, I am not crying; it's just that a tiny particle of dirt got into my eye."

When I was old enough to understand the intricate complexities of life, I formed a reason in my mind as to why she cried. I believe she truly felt the hardships of life and the heavy burden of raising eight children with a husband having no permanent job, no money in the bank, no real assets, and very little education. I thought she truly felt hopeless and disillusioned about how to provide for her children so we could have a future.

CHAPTER 2

Being Resourceful about Food

I LEARNED EARLY on of the various ways I could be of help to my family. When I was about ten years old, my father made me a fish trap, which is a round basket made of bamboo with a wide, open bottom and a smaller opening at the top to pull out a trapped fish. He also made me a bamboo hamper, which I tied around my waist and kept all the fish I'd collected in.

On most weekends, my childhood friends and I would go fishing at a nearby rice field with shallow water around noontime, when the weather was the warmest. It was at this time of the day that the fish tended to rest under the shades of the rice plants. We knew their resting places because the water where they would rest and hide would always be very dark and murky. On any given fishing day, I would usually bring home six to seven mudfish of varying sizes.

During the corn harvest season, my friends and I would help the farmers manually separate each ear of corn from the cornstalk and pile the ears onto a cart pulled by a water buffalo. Whenever we finished the task for each cornfield, the farmer would usually award each of us with about four ears of corn. After a day's work, each of us would bring home twelve to fourteen ears of corn.

Whenever I came home with fish, corn, or other things to eat, I was always greeted by the unmistakable delight on my mother's face. I knew she very much appreciated my resourcefulness in being able to contribute to our family's dire situation. When I was a young boy, it always touched my heart.

Another enjoyable childhood activity involved collecting an edible brownish beetle-like flying insect that usually appeared during late afternoon in a nearby cornfield adjacent to a river. The gathering of these insects happened around mid-April of each year, when the corn began flowering. The females were easily determined by their bigger and rounder bellies. Whenever a female attempted to fly away, perhaps its scent attracted the attention of several males whose intention was to mate with the female. When three or four males would fly very close to a female and position themselves on her back, that was the signal for me to grab them.

I also recalled that whenever those insects were part of the meal, my young siblings and I would play with their cut-off heads by lining them up next to each other in something similar to a soldier formation. Growing up with lots of siblings gave us some really enjoyable times together, always playing with each other, eating and praying together, and making the best with what we had.

Another enjoyable, but very difficult, childhood endeavor was catching the big rice field frogs, which resembled bullfrogs. To catch them, we would use a five-foot bamboo stick similar to a fishing pole. We put a string at the end of the stick with an earthworm tied to it as bait without a hook. Once a frog bit the worm, we immediately hauled it up and dropped it into a deep burlap bag held high enough by the left hand.

Similarly, snails I had caught from the rice fields, cooked with coconut milk mixed with ginger and fresh yam leaves, were also delectable. The modern equivalent of such a snail meal is widely known as "escargot," which is served nowadays in restaurants worldwide.

CHAPTER 3

Supporting a Large Family

IN ORDER TO provide for a large family of eight children, my father ventured into the buying and selling of anything that he believed could yield him some profit. The first business venture he tried involved buying three or four very young water buffalo. After school, it would be the job of my brother and me to take the water buffalo to the meadow for pasture. After having their fill, we would take them to the nearby river for bathing and drinking.

My brother and I quickly became proficient in riding the water buffalo, using a burlap sack as our saddle. A number of times we rode the water buffalo standing on their backs while holding onto the rope tied around the horns that was used for guiding the animal.

Most afternoons on the way to the meadow, we would have a race with both of us yelling "Hyah, hyah," pretending to be American cowboys, while hitting the side of the animal with a rope, which made the water buffalo run faster.

The daily green pasturing for at least four months was required in order to achieve the ultimate goal, which was to fatten the water buffalo before selling them. As part of the preparation-to-sell ordeal, and at least a few weeks before a planned sale, my father would shave the back and the sides of each water buffalo.

After a few days, their hair would start to regrow, which brought tremendous pain on our rear ends as the short hair was very sharp and coarse, and easily penetrated our sack saddles. To alleviate the pain, we would put small pillows underneath the burlap sack to serve as a cushion.

The second business venture my father got involved with was the buying of large quantities of ducks—by the thousands. Again, similar to the water buffalo, the objective was to fatten the ducks then sell them, as well as their eggs, for a good profit. While the ducks were in a makeshift fenced-in area in our backyard, it was my job to collect the eggs every morning. After having duck eggs as part of most of our meals for five or six weeks straight, we became tired of eating them and told our mother to give at least some of the eggs to our neighbors.

The third business venture, as I recall, involved buying a mango grove. By making his own thorough assessment of each mango tree, my father would estimate the number of bushels of mangoes that could be harvested from each tree. He would then submit a proposal to buy all the fruits from the entire mango grove at a certain price for that particular harvest season. He would then sell the mangoes wholesale to large store owners at a reasonable profit.

My mother told us later on that our father did make good money in most of his business dealings, including their eventual ownership of a few hectares of rice fields. That was evident by the fact that they were able to send us all to college, except for one sibling who decided to attend a dressmaking vocational school after grade school.

Early on, and on many occasions, my parents ingrained in our heads the importance of education. As they often said, education would be our only salvation since they were not in a position to offer us any financial inheritance.

My father emphasized often enough the benefits of higher education, saying, "There are only a few ways by which you can conquer poverty. The most effective way is through education. Just look at me. I don't want any of you to wind up doing what I do."

Even though my father was a third-grade dropout, I considered him to be a principled, well-learned man whose ways of thinking and living were molded by his life experiences.

We all knew the hardships our parents endured for so many years and the sacrifices they made, depriving themselves of many things. They saved as much as they could in order to support us, and they made sure that we finished our college educations. During those hard and long years, I never saw my parents go to see a movie or go out to eat at a local restaurant. They bought new clothes and shoes only on rare special occasions. My father had not experienced driving or owning a car.

CHAPTER 4

Early School Life

MY EXPERIENCES DURING my remaining childhood years continued to be marked by daily struggles and hardships. I attended a local public grade school by the name of Makinabang Elementary School. For the whole time I was in attendance at that school, I walked to and from school without shoes, about a half hour's walk each way.

I usually went home for lunch around noon time when the heat of the day was at its peak. That was the most agonizing experience for me as the asphalt on the road would start to melt and I could no longer walk on it without shoes. Walking on the side of the road was not an easy feat either since both sides had small stones that were sharp and hot.

On most days, my friends and I would run as fast as possible just to shorten the time we had to endure the heat and pain. For some reason, we were able to adapt. We were able to keep that up for six long years.

My grade school days, though filled with many challenges, also had their fun, enjoyable, and proud moments. It was during fifth grade that I was selected to play first base in Little League baseball, which was very enjoyable to me. We traveled from town to town to participate in inter-elementary school Little League baseball competitions. The farthest we traveled was to Subic Bay in Olongapo, Zambales, which was about three hundred fifty miles away from my hometown.

Our team was selected from among hundreds of Little League teams within the province of Bulacan to play against a team of American players. The opposing team was made up of the children of soldiers in the US Air Force stationed in that particular region. I noticed that the American Little League players wore very nice uniforms and that their baseball field was immaculate.

Halfway to the destination, our team stopped near a soda-manufacturing facility to have lunch. As a young boy, I had an insatiable curiosity. I remember asking our coach how the machine was able to fill all the empty bottles with soda to the exact same level without any spillover and at a rapid pace. Almost at the same time I was asking him the question, I also observed that one of the workers was on the phone talking to somebody.

Again, overly inquisitive, I asked my coach how a phone could transmit a voice conversation over long distances. Without answering, and irked by my questions, or perhaps not knowing the answer, he said to me in a rather sarcastic voice, "You ask too many questions, wise guy."

It was during my grade school graduation that I truly felt very proud. At that particular event, the local dignitaries were all on the stage, along with my father, who at the time was the barrio captain. Such an event was usually attended by hundreds of people, including parents, siblings, neighbors, and other guests. That graduation night, I was wearing my best outfit. I was also wearing leather shoes for the first time.

After singing the Philippine national anthem and watching a local folk-dance performance, the principal declared that he would call to the stage the students who had achieved academic honors. But before doing so, however, he mentioned the school's decision to recognize first the student who was given the very difficult task of opening all the classroom doors and windows very early each morning and locking them after school hours.

He said, "The entire faculty and staff, along with the principal, has decided to grant the Most Helpful Boy Award to Rodrigo T. Gabriel." On my way to the stage to get the award, my father stood up and hugged me.

The principal went on, calling the names of those being awarded with academic honors. He first called the students who had earned an honorable mention, and then he called the last student receiving the valedictorian award. At one point in the ceremony he said, "The student with academic honor receiving the third honorable mention award is Rodrigo T. Gabriel."

On my way up to the stage for the second time, I could hear the principal's comments to my father: "Mr. Gabriel, your son is not only a very helpful boy but also is one of the smartest students. You must be very proud of him."

I did hear my father's response: "I am indeed very proud of him."

CHAPTER 5

Life in the Metropolitan City

MEANWHILE, MY HIGH school experience was somewhat uneventful, with one exception: it was the place where I first met my future wife, Sylvia. Being that I attended high school in Manila, the capital city of the Philippines, most students generally came from families with much greater financial means than my family.

The city boys, I eventually found out, were more advanced in many ways than the boys from the province. Some of my freshman classmates wore long pants, fancy blue jeans, and expensive sneakers. Some students, like me, because of financial constraints, still wore khaki shorts. I only started wearing long pants at the beginning of my junior year.

Being away from home for the first time, I quickly realized that my resiliency was being tested again. During the first two years of being away from my parents, I was missing them very much, especially my mother. I really missed her cooking, her constant guidance and advice, and her motherly love and support. Not being with her caused me to cry most nights. I missed my mother so much that when I was alone in the apartment, I would talk to the birds chirping outside up in the trees, asking them to say hello to my mother for me.

They reminded me of my pet bird, similar to a raven, which I had raised up since it was just a few weeks old. As it grew older, the bird would always stay close to me. At times it would make some chirping noise as if it were calling my name. Out of loneliness for my mother, I wrote the word *Inang* (meaning "Mom") in big letters on the inside of the front door to my apartment, a testament that I missed her very much and longed for her to be with me.

With two older sisters and a cousin, who had just started work as an engineer with an electric company, we could only afford a one-bedroom apartment in downtown Manila, which was a half hour's walk to my school, named the Philippine College of Commerce, High School Department (also known as PCC High School). My parents had decided to enroll me in that high school because it was a reputable vocational public school with very low tuition. The school offered some vocational courses, such as stenography and typing; some marketing courses; and bookkeeping. During the early days, those were some of the basic skills needed to quickly find an entry-level job.

Our arrangement in the apartment was such that my cousin was sharing the rent. My oldest sister told me that the least we could do to help our cousin was to prepare breakfast for him since he had to leave very early for work with an almost two-hour commute. Since both my sisters also worked full time, they said they needed to have a good night's sleep. I was therefore assigned the task of waking up at 5:00 in the morning to prepare breakfast for my cousin, which consisted mainly of making coffee, frying two eggs, and buttering a roll. I handled that task religiously for almost two years. I was thirteen and fourteen years old at that time, the age when most kids would be sound asleep at such an early hour. However, I learned early on from my parents the importance of hard work and responsibility, so such a task did not bother me at all.

It was during my junior year that I found myself enjoying high school life. I began to develop friendships with my classmates. They would take me to dinner dance parties. I learned how to dance the twist, the mashed potato, and the boogie, and I participated in the recreational games of basketball and baseball. I had pretty much adjusted to the lifestyle of a metropolitan city.

However, toward the end of the last semester of my senior year, my father said to me, "Perhaps adjusting to city life caused you to spend more time partying than studying. That's why you did not get any honors award this time."

In retrospect, I realized that I had let him down. It left me with a terrible feeling of disappointment. I did learn a hard lesson from my high school experience. I promised myself to do much better in college.

CHAPTER 6

College Life and Work Experiences

COLLEGE LIFE AT the Philippine College of Commerce, on the other hand, was more enjoyable for me than the high school experience. During my freshman and sophomore years, I was selected to play college baseball as a first baseman and was awarded the usual partial athletic scholarship. Our team did a lot of traveling to compete against different colleges within Manila and neighboring cities. We became very good friends with other athletes who played other sports.

However, it was during my junior year that I decided to transfer to a bigger college, Mapua Institute of Technology (MIT), also located in downtown Manila. MIT offered courses in engineering as well as business administration courses with majors such as accounting, banking, and finance. The student population at MIT was about five thousand at that time, which was roughly double the size of my prior college.

My plan was to focus on business administration courses, majoring in finance and banking. My decision to change colleges was motivated by my desire to work full time and continue my studies at night. It was around that time that two of my siblings were also in college. I could sense the financial difficulty that my parents were undergoing.

It was in the last semester of my junior year that I landed a full-time clerical job at a relatively big industrial firm with a few subsidiary companies that manufactured various products such as sneakers, steel, fertilizer, and small fishing boats. By having a full-time job, I was able to contribute to my family's expenses as I paid for most of my college tuition, even though balancing work and school proved to be very difficult at times.

But I persevered relentlessly and really did my best both in college and at my job while remaining strongly committed to my faith and daily prayers. It was in my senior year that I was awarded partial academic scholarships for maintaining at least a 3.5 GPA, which therefore lowered my tuition.

It was also during senior year that I decided to enter the student government. I was elected chairman of the Senior Assembly. In that capacity, I participated in various intercollegiate workshops and conferences pertinent to enhancing students' involvement in the formulation of college policies and the setting of educational standards. The experience provided me with the opportunity to be recognized with certain distinction by both the professors and the students.

After completing my undergraduate studies, I started a new full-time job in the accounting department of a private development corporation for a couple of years, while taking MBA courses in finance and taxation at night. That was my first exposure to international finance as that company was a quasi-government entity whose main line of business was to secure borrowings from the International Bank for Reconstruction and Development (IBRD) in consultation with the International Monetary Fund (IMF).

The funds received from IBRD would then be used in supporting and lending to new and developing small manufacturing industries around the Philippines. Afterward, I ventured into sales and marketing for a year at a British company selling plastic neon signs, which, at that time, was the latest trend in outdoor commercial signs.

CHAPTER 7

A Year of Courtship

SEVERAL MONTHS AFTER college graduation, my best friend from high school and I went to a birthday party uninvited, although my friend was an acquaintance of the celebrant. It was at that party that I had another encounter with my future wife, Sylvia. I immediately started a conversation with her. I vividly remember my first comment to her, which was, "You look quite familiar to me. Did you attend high school at PCC High?" She quickly responded, "Yes, I did."

We had a very long and enjoyable conversation about our high school days, college life in general, and our experiences related to work. I found out that she had graduated from the University of the East and had just passed the Certified Public Accountant (CPA) board examination. I somehow sensed a certain spark in the way we talked to each other, and I knew we had a mutual interest to learn more about each other. That particular chance meeting led us to agree to see each other again sometime soon.

During high school, Sylvia and I had really no eventful interaction with each other, not only because we belonged to different sections, but also because during those early high school years, teenagers generally did not engage in any form of serious relationship with the opposite sex. However, seeing her again after more than five years as a mature, sophisticated, and confident woman definitely stirred a part of me to develop an attraction to her.

One Saturday afternoon, my college buddy and I decided to visit Sylvia's apartment in the town of San Juan, a suburb of Manila. I immediately sensed a certain happiness in her smiling face upon seeing me. That pleasant afternoon was followed by a couple of weekend visits at her new house in Mandaluyong, another suburban township.

It was around November of 1968 when I started the serious courtship of Sylvia. Back then, the courtship process, similar to the early stages of dating today, was very conservative. It involved going to the young woman's house every Saturday afternoon, which would usually start around 5:00 and end about 8:30 p.m.

During the initial stage of the courtship, while Sylvia and I would usually sit outside on the front porch of her house, I would observe that her father would always be watching TV in the living room adjacent to the porch. The living room was just a few feet away from the porch, separated by a glass door. The unspoken rule of this type of conservative courtship was that the suitor was not supposed to hold the young woman's hand in front of her parents. There was to be no dating and no expectation of a dinner invitation until reaching the formal boyfriend–girlfriend stage.

There were a few times when I had to extend my stay just a bit, particularly when I noticed that Sylvia's father had fallen asleep while watching TV. During those few times, what I considered to be unguarded precious moments, I would nervously reach out and hold Sylvia's hand for a minute or two, which always gave me a warm and energetic feeling, a feeling that lingered as I made the almost two-hour trip back home.

It was after a year of courtship that we both fell for each other and her parents and siblings gradually noticed that our relationship was getting really serious. Soon after, for the first time, I was invited by her parents to have dinner with them. At the dinner table, as I sat next to Sylvia with her parents and several of her siblings sitting around us, I felt awkward. I began to sweat as it seemed like everybody was watching my every move. Such a feeling, however, disappeared as soon as I felt a sincere welcome from them. Her parents confirmed their sincerity, saying to me, "Please feel at home and just help yourself."

Following that dinner, Sylvia's parents gave us permission to formally date. During the subsequent weekends, instead of having conversation on her porch, we would go to a nearby mall and see a movie, followed by dinner outside, the occasional stroll in the park, and sometimes go to a friend's party together.

After several months of being considered boyfriend and girlfriend, I began gradually introducing Sylvia to my family. There was one occasion when my sister went with me and Sylvia to a party in a town about eighty miles south of Manila. That was followed by a family get-together, a river picnic, where we had lunch in a small wooden boat in my hometown.

It was in late September of 1969 when Sylvia and I decided to inform her parents of our plan to get married in the following year. Just as soon as they heard of our plan, both her parents began crying.

Sylvia's father posed a question to her, saying, "What about your plan to go to America?"

Sylvia gave him a reassuring response, saying, "My plan has not changed. We will eventually settle in America as it has been my earnest desire and a lifelong dream to go to America."

CHAPTER 8

Married Life and the Birth of Our First Daughter

IN SEPTEMBER OF 1970, Sylvia and I got married at the Pope Pius II church, not too far from downtown Manila. Our wedding was attended by almost two hundred guests from both sides of the family, followed by a reception at Sylvia's house in Mandaluyong. It was certainly one of the happiest moments of my life.

We chose Baguio city, the summer capital of the Philippines, as the location for our honeymoon. That was my first trip to that city, and I was quite impressed by the cool weather and the cleanliness of the streets. We went for a boat ride in a lake situated in the middle of a big park surrounded by lots of greenery and pine trees. The local residents seemed very friendly and hospitable. Most of the restaurant food was delicious with lots of fresh vegetables and was very reasonably priced. We really had an enjoyable and memorable stay in Baguio city.

A few days after getting back from our honeymoon, Sylvia's parents suggested that since it was our plan to go to America at the soonest possible time, perhaps we should stay temporarily at their house instead of renting an apartment. We accepted their generous offer, and since both Sylvia and I had relatively good full-time jobs, we offered to share in the household expenses, such as their monthly mortgage and the groceries. Her parents were very appreciative of our contributions.

During one of our weekend visits to my parents, my father pulled me aside. He and I sat in one corner of the house while Sylvia was talking to my mother.

He started to quietly give me another bit of fatherly advice, saying, "Son, now that you are married and staying with your in-laws, always try to do your best not to have any shortcomings in your relationship with them as they are not your true blood family." He added, "And you do not have to worry about us as much. We will be alright."

In the summer of the following year, Sylvia gave birth to our first child, a girl. We decided to name her Bernadette after the patron Saint Bernadette of Lourdes, who was the focal point during a religious retreat that Sylvia attended. We nicknamed her Bernie.

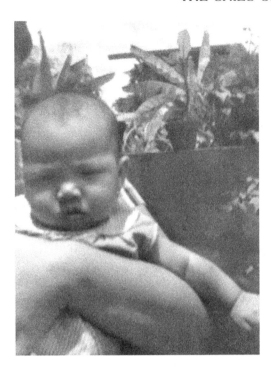

Over the next several months, our family life became quite hectic. We would wake up very early each morning to prepare all the things that our daughter needed for the day. Since both Sylvia and I worked full time, my mother-in-law served as Bernadette's primary caretaker for several months.

My last job in the Philippines, before immigrating to the United States, was with a large soda bottling company. I had started out as a route salesman, and after just a couple of years, I was promoted to a sales supervisor position at its sister company, another bottling company with a different brand. I was twenty-six years old at that time, and there were ten route salesmen under my supervision who were much older than I.

It was a very challenging position with lots of responsibilities involving working extra hours, conducting weekly meetings, attending supervisory seminars, and making regular visits to large wholesale outlets. In every job that I held, I always took the advice of my father to heart, which was to work a lot harder and a lot smarter than the others, always to think outside the box, and to be a problem-solver.

During my first year as a supervisor, my team consistently led in sales production. The senior management eventually noticed my team's excellent performance, as well as the apparent effectiveness of my leadership. At a later date, it was made known to me by the sales trainees that during some of the sales training seminars, the general manager of the company praised me for my leadership and told the trainees that they should consider me as their role model and that they should emulate my work ethic.

After just one year as a supervisor, and at the relatively young age of twenty-seven, I was informed by the senior management of the parent company that they were seriously considering me for the position of general manager at their Davao City plant. At that time, Davao City was one of the up-and-coming big cities in the southern region of the Philippines.

However, it was also during that time when Sylvia and I received a letter from the US Embassy office in Manila informing us that the immigration application filed by Sylvia way before our marriage had just been approved. The approval automatically included her immediate family, such as her husband and any children. The letter stipulated that we had only six months to make a decision.

On separate occasions, we immediately consulted both our parents. After several conversations with them, they offered pretty much the same advice to us, namely to try a new life in America. My father-in-law mentioned the very good and positive things about the United States and the many employment opportunities for college graduates like us.

Both our parents had also warned us of the potential difficulty it would pose being apart from each other, which could lead to a possible strain on my and Sylvia's relationship considering that we'd only been married for a year at that time.

They also emphasized that we must give the utmost consideration to the well-being of our firstborn baby, who was just six months old. My parents further inquired as to who will take care of Bernadette while we're both out looking for jobs.

They suggested leaving our daughter in the care of my single sister, Soledad, who had volunteered to help babysit for other family members. Once Sylvia and I both had secured stable jobs, our parents emphasized that we could surely come back to the Philippines to take our daughter with us back to America.

My father pulled me aside and said, "Son, now that you may be going to a very far place, I would like to give you some parting advice, which might perhaps be my last piece of advice to you." My father was seventy-six years old when Sylvia and I left the Philippines to immigrate to the United States. He went on to say, "Son, wherever you go and whatever you do in life, please remember that the true measure of a man's success is not how much wealth, power, or material things he has accumulated over his lifetime; it is measured by how many good deeds he has done for his fellow men." Deep in my heart, I believed strongly in the merit of that advice. I have incorporated it as part of my life's philosophy ever since.

I also had an intimate conversation with my in-laws, which was heartwarming, very pleasant, and encouraging. My mother-in-law said, "During your almost two years of being married to our daughter, we have witnessed that you have been a very responsible husband and a very generous human being. We consider you heaven's gift to our family."

I almost cried upon hearing that as I was filled with joy and gratification. The thought of my father's advice concerning my relationship with my in-laws weighed heavily on my mind at that very moment.

CHAPTER 9

Life in America: New Beginnings

SYLVIA AND I truly had a very difficult decision to make. There were many nights when I agonized over what was best for all of us. Even though deep in our hearts we did not want to leave our baby daughter Bernadette in the Philippines, after evaluating all the different aspects and options, we had decided to try a new life in America.

At the airport while saying goodbye to everybody, we were all crying. My and Sylvia's hearts were truly broken while kissing and hugging our daughter. Once we were seated in the airplane, people could see that we were both sobbing like children.

Since we did not have enough money to pay for the airline tickets, we had applied for an airline program called the Fly Now, Pay Later plan, the fares payable within two years. As I recall, we left Manila with only two small pieces of luggage and about three hundred fifty dollars in our pocket.

We first landed on US soil on February 6, 1972. Upon arrival, we stayed with my brother, Dominador, in a one-bedroom apartment in

Newark, New Jersey, where we remained for about six months. My brother and his friend slept in the living room, letting us stay in the bedroom. The next day after our arrival, we immediately went to several employment agencies in New York City with a bunch of résumés in hand.

Sylvia and I were both excited to see the famous city of New York (known as the financial center of the world) for the first time. We saw the large crowds on the streets and the almost bumper-to-bumper lines of cars and taxicabs on the very noisy roadways. We were also in awe of the many towering skyscrapers, some of them world-renowned and considered historical, such as the Empire State Building, the Chrysler Building, Grand Central Station, the World Trade Center, and Saint Patrick's Cathedral.

Since it was winter season at the time, while walking the streets of Manhattan, I noticed that my shoes were shrinking and beginning to get really wet inside from the snow. They were of course made in the Philippines with material suited for warm weather. Moreover, my socks were also getting soaked, and the sides of my shoes were accumulating whitish powder from the snow. It was quickly becoming very uncomfortable to walk with shrinking shoes, not to mention embarrassing going to job interviews with very wet shoes.

After several more job interviews that had been arranged by the employment agencies, our perseverance paid off. After just a couple of weeks, we were both fortunate enough to have found our first jobs. I landed an administrative/clerical job with a nonprofit national banking trade organization based in New York City. My primary responsibility was to maintain and update the membership database. Sylvia took a job as an accounting clerk with an insurance company located in Newark, New Jersey. She was mostly responsible for processing the accounts receivables and payables.

Since we did not have any work experience locally, we had to start at a very meager salary. However, thanks to our disciplined frugality, and with two sources of income, we were able to pay the airline company within a year. We were also able to help pay the monthly rent, and we had started sending some money to my sister Soledad, who was caring for our daughter back in the Philippines.

Sylvia and I both made a strong commitment to work very hard and save as much as we could in order to afford a trip back to the Philippines as soon as possible to see our daughter and to take her with us back to America. We closely monitored our expenses, only purchased the necessities, took the bus and train to work, rarely ate out, washed our clothes by hand, walked to the grocery stores, and cut our own hair. Having the occasional dinner out at the local Burger King was considered a big treat for us.

In the course of our first two years in the United States, there was rarely a night when we did not cry. Missing our daughter very much, we regularly made long-distance calls to the Philippines just to hear her voice and her childish giggles. Right after hanging up the phone each time, we would always find ourselves crying even more.

During those initial two years, we thought many times of going back home to the Philippines as our life in America was full of sacrifices, deep loneliness, the challenges of adapting to a new culture, and the dissatisfaction of doing menial jobs. We questioned ourselves at times, wondering if we had made the right decision. On many occasions, we felt that we were just existing and not truly living as our life was plainly boring, doing the same daily routine with painful hardships and sacrifices and being so far away from our loved ones. It was truly a test of determination, endurance, and resiliency.

But the thought of providing a better future for our daughter weighed heavily in our minds, and we wanted to prove to our respective families that we had made the right decision. Deep in our hearts, we also wanted to be successful in America so as to make them proud of us.

Continuing to work very hard at our jobs, we saved as much as we could, prayed a lot, cried together a lot, and persevered, very determined to overcome all those obstacles with the ultimate goal of bringing our daughter back with us to the USA at the soonest possible time.

At the end of the second year, we both felt that we had enough savings, so we decided to set up a plan for the next course of action. We each approached our respective employers and told them of our situation, requesting a three-month leave of absence without pay. Fortunately, our employers understood our situation, and perhaps partly attributable to our work performances, they agreed to give us the requested leaves of absence.

CHAPTER 10

Trip Back to the Philippines

SO OFF WE went back to the Philippines in late February of 1974, with one goal in mind: to bring our daughter back with us to the US and be together again as a family. We took lots of toys, chocolates, and clothes back home for her, including a life-sized Barbie doll. Bernadette was two and a half years old at that time. Upon landing at the Manila airport, we felt great joy and excitement to be with our daughter again.

Lots of relatives from both sides of the family were at the airport, welcoming us with hugs and kisses. When it was our turn to hug and kiss our daughter, she turned away and stayed in the hands of my sister Soledad, her caretaker. Of course, Bernadette did not recognize us. We knew it would take a long time to become close to her again and gain her trust.

Bernadette called my sister "Mama," and all along she really thought that my sister was her mother. But being with our daughter again after two long years, even though she did not recognize us yet, gave us a feeling of great happiness as well as heartfelt gratitude that God had granted us such a special occasion.

Both our parents were very happy to see us again as evidenced by the shared tears of joy and overwhelming elation. On separate occasions, we shared some private moments with our parents. My parents first inquired about our life in America.

I began by saying that given the prevailing currency exchange rate, the dollar had a very high value compared to the Philippine peso. And even though our salaries were not much, our work was still relatively financially rewarding, especially when the dollar was to be spent in the Philippines. However, I also indicated that our life in the United States was not devoid of hardships and sacrifices.

We mentioned our living conditions, a one-bedroom apartment in a four-story building with ten units on each floor, saying that we knew only very few of the tenants. And because we could only afford a certain amount in rent, our apartment's location was not in a very good neighborhood and we rarely opened the windows, even in the daytime. We also touched on our feeling of loneliness, saying that we deeply missed our daughter and both our families. Furthermore, our adjustment to a different culture continued to evolve, and doing routinely tedious jobs could be frustrating at times.

I went on to say that in the beginning, because of our heavy accents, there were quite a number of times when our conversations with Americans, whether at work or somewhere else, were not very pleasant as we had to repeat ourselves a few times before they could fully understand us. Furthermore, assimilating into a new culture was also challenging at the outset, but we were trying our best to gradually adjust to it.

On the business side, however, I mentioned the ingenuity and the unparalleled smart vision of the American businessmen who had established the largest and most successful companies in the world. I could sense the intense enthusiasm of my father to hear more about the American way of life and the historical events leading to the United States' becoming the most powerful nation on earth as evidenced by its economic and military might.

My father, who had neither traveled outside the Philippines nor flown on an airplane, was amazed upon learning of the United States' spectacular achievements in the medical field, along with its computer innovations, putting a man in the moon, and achieving dominance in automobile and steel manufacturing, all while providing generous and significant aid to struggling countries around the world.

After hearing about all our hardships and sacrifices, as well as the nice and inspiring things about America, my father sat closer to me and, in his usual measured voice, said, "Son, please remember that it is during times of difficulty and adversity that the true character of a person is best revealed." He went on to say, "What is more important is not how many times you failed and were disappointed, but how you are able to rise up each time and overcome life's obstacles and challenges." Throughout my life's journey, and with undeniable certainty, such invaluable advice would again ring true as greater adversity was to come later on in my life.

My mother added her own motherly advice, saying to both of us, "No matter how busy you are, you must never forget to say your prayers before you go to sleep. And please know that even though you are far away from us, I am always praying for all of you."

My mother was indeed a very kind woman whose utmost care and devotion to our family was unquestionably her life's purpose. Throughout my entire life, she never raised her voice toward us. Her calm demeanor, even during bad times, undoubtedly strengthened us. She was relatively small in stature with a soft, soothing voice, but she always had an aura of sincere concern, unconditional love, and care whenever she was around us.

CHAPTER 11

Reunion with Bernadette

WHILE BACK IN the Philippines, Sylvia and I spent most of our time in my parents' house, where my sister Soledad performed the daily chores of caring for Bernadette. We played with our daughter a lot, took her to several shopping malls, went to different places with her, slept close to her, took turns helping to feed and bathe her. We were truly enjoying being together, starting to laugh with one another, hugging and kissing each other, and occasionally crying together.

After a long while, we observed that Bernadette was gradually warming up to us. We could sense that she was beginning to feel comfortable with us being around her. Soledad was also helping in the process by mentioning to Bernadette, at the appropriate times, that we are her biological parents. But at two and a half years old, Bernadette, we knew, could not yet comprehend that.

We knew we had limited time to bond with her, but we also knew that it was something we could not rush. The one thing that we definitely did not want to do was to cause any kind of traumatic experience for her. Gradual and steady progress toward developing a closer bond with her in the most comforting and trusting way for her was definitely our ultimate goal.

Toward the end of the third month of our trip to the Philippines, I started to prepare to go back to the USA to resume my work. It was again a very difficult time as I was leaving Bernadette for the second time. Everybody in the family was crying again, although this time I knew it would be a short period of temporary separation.

Since we believed that we had not yet developed the bond we sought with our daughter, Sylvia decided to extend her stay in the Philippines for another month so she could be with Bernadette a little bit longer, hoping that the two of them would become a lot more comfortable with each other. We knew, however, that such an extension could potentially pose a problem for Sylvia's employer. So just as soon as I settled back in my work, I immediately called her employer and informed them of the situation. Unfortunately, they indicated that they could not allow a month's extension as they needed somebody to do her work, which was already piling up. When I relayed the message to Sylvia through a long-distance phone call, I could sense disappointment in her voice. But we both agreed that her mission to get closer to Bernadette was definitely a lot more important than keeping a job.

As the end of the fourth month was fast approaching, we had to think about how we could convince Bernadette to join us in the States. My parents suggested a strategy whereby Sylvia would take Bernadette to go shopping at a place far away and allegedly meet Soledad at the shopping mall. That seemed the only solution since they knew it would be very difficult to separate Bernadette from Soledad since they were always used to being around each other.

One day, while Bernadette was sound asleep, Sylvia slowly carried her into the car and drove away toward my in-laws' house in Mandaluyong, a suburb of Manila. However, about halfway to their destination, Bernadette woke up. Her first question was, "Where's my mama?"

Sylvia responded in a very convincing way, saying, "We are on our way to meet your mama in the mall to buy some dresses for you." Bernadette, showing no signs of apprehension, eventually fell asleep again.

As they were getting closer to my in-laws' house, Bernadette woke up and asked the same question many times: "Where's my mama?"

Sylvia's response was, "We're on our way to see her."

The following morning, just as soon as Bernadette woke up, she started to cry and again, asking, "Where's my mama?"

Sylvia's consistent response was "She is coming soon."

Another strategy employed by Sylvia was to ask her cousins to bring their young children over so they could play with Bernadette. Being occupied playing with other children, Bernadette stopped asking about her "mama," at least temporarily. Sylvia tried very hard, using all kinds of tactics, such as taking Bernadette to see several cartoon movies, taking her to the local zoo, buying her more toys, ice cream, chocolates, dresses, shoes, and so forth, and really taking care of her every want and need.

After a few more weeks of being together every day and every night, Bernadette was asking less and less about her mama. For the first time in a long time, she called Sylvia "Mommy." The hardest test, however, was when it was time for the two of them to travel back to America.

A large number of relatives, including most of my siblings, were at the airport saying their goodbyes to Sylvia and Bernadette. Everybody was again crying while hugging each other. The time of parting from loved ones was always very difficult and emotionally draining.

Sylvia told me later on that Soledad was also at the airport. She saw Bernadette from a distance, but she made sure that Bernadette did not see her. According to Sylvia, she saw my sister also crying really hard. We both knew that it was quite difficult for her to be separated from Bernadette as they naturally had developed a very close bond with each other during those two and a half years of a mother-and-child kind of relationship.

CHAPTER 12

Back to America with Bernadette

FINALLY, DURING THE late summer of 1974, Sylvia and Bernadette arrived in Jersey City, New Jersey. We continued to stay in that one-bedroom apartment in Jersey City for almost two years. Over the next few months, however, Sylvia decided not to look for a job yet and instead stayed with Bernadette. She would take her to the babysitter, who lived just one floor below our apartment, for two days a week. She did this over the next several weeks so Bernadette could familiarize herself with the babysitter, who was also caring for a few other children almost the same age as Bernadette.

The other kids were born in the United States, so they were starting to speak in English, while Bernadette spoke only Tagalog (the Philippine national language). It was amazing to observe the kids adapting pretty quickly to the environment and getting along with each other despite the language barrier. We observed the daily progressive adjustments demonstrated by Bernadette. By the fourth week, she began to speak a few words in English.

Almost three months of being together in the apartment, with Bernadette beginning to show more enthusiasm for going to the babysitter's place every other day provided some encouragement for

Sylvia to start looking for a job. Fortunately, it was around that time that a neighbor mentioned that his company was looking to hire and that there were a couple of vacancies in their accounting department.

He asked Sylvia for a copy of her résumé, to be forwarded to their human resources department. Her résumé highlighted her relevant background, given her bachelor's degree in accounting and CPA certification from the Philippines. After a few weeks, she got the good news from our neighbor that she was being offered a job in the accounting department of the investment brokerage firm, located in downtown Manhattan.

We were both very happy about the good news, and at the same time we were very worried and sad because we knew we had to leave Bernadette at the babysitter's place five days a week. Over the next three months, Bernadette would cry every morning when we would leave her at the babysitter's.

We would go down together to the main gate each morning, and Bernadette would be crying really hard, saying, "Mommy, stay with me. Please don't leave, Mommy." She would say the same exact words several times every morning for several weeks. The babysitter, hearing her pleadings, would go down to the main gate with the other kids, and all of them would try to console Bernadette.

Each morning on our way out of the apartment, Sylvia and I were both very sad, heartbroken at the sight of Bernadette crying and pleading. Not a single day passed at the office that we did not think of her. On many occasions, we tried very hard to hold back our tears. We would already be at our respective offices, but in our heads we could still hear Bernadette's crying voice, which naturally brought immense sadness to our hearts.

However, around the middle of the third month, Bernadette had gradually adjusted to the daily routine, and her morning crying occurred less and less. Bernadette stayed with the same babysitter for almost two years, after which time we transferred her to a nearby pre-K program operated by a group of Catholic nuns.

The objective of enrolling her into a pre-K program was twofold: Bernadette would receive daily care similar to what the babysitter provided, and at the same time, she and the other kids would be provided pre-K instructions. As expected, during the initial five or six weeks of the program, Bernadette would cry a lot as it was another new environment she had to adjust to.

The nuns were very strict in their regimented activities that employed disciplinary actions. At a very young age, Bernadette learned how to behave properly. Then she started to learn how to draw, put together some simple sentences, and do some minor arithmetic. She started to adjust nicely.

CHAPTER 13

The Birth of Our Second Daughter

IT WAS DURING the early spring of 1976, which was about four years from the time we had first arrived in America, when we bought and moved into our first house, a two-family residence in the Greenville section of Jersey City. Such good news was preceded by another bit of good news as Sylvia was expecting another baby girl.

Our second daughter, Melissa Mae (nicknamed Lis), was born in late May of 1976. We decorated the room where Melissa would be sleeping with pink ribbons around her crib, pink pillows and blankets, and lots of balloons all around the room. Bernadette, who was almost five years old at that time, was very much looking forward to being with her baby sister.

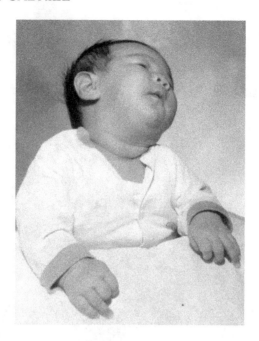

However, our anticipation and excitement were diminished by the news from the doctor that Melissa and Sylvia could not go home yet because of the yellow discoloration of her skin, also known as jaundice, caused by a high bilirubin count. The doctor stated that Melissa would remain in the hospital for at least three days for photo therapy, putting her under a special blue light to help reduce bilirubin levels. The three days of waiting seemed very long and was very worrisome for us since we were not quite sure what to expect. We were hoping and praying hard that everything would be fine with Melissa's health.

After the third day, the doctor called to inform us that the jaundice was gone and that Melissa could go home. Bernadette and I immediately rushed to the hospital and picked up Melissa. Bernadette was very happy and excited. While the three of them were huddled together in the back seat, I observed that Bernadette was holding her baby sister's hand all the way home.

Once we got settled at home, we gathered around Melissa with tears in our eyes while gratefully praying to God, thanking Him that we were finally together as a family. The good news about Melissa being allowed to go home was preceded by more good news regarding my job.

After almost three years of doing basically clerical work, I was promoted to an accountant position with more challenging responsibilities and with an adjustment in pay. Meanwhile, for the next three months of being settled in our first house, Sylvia and our two young girls were really enjoying each other every day. Melissa was gradually getting bigger. She was also starting to smile occasionally.

When Melissa was not sleeping, Bernadette always wanted to be with her. Sylvia would occasionally let Bernadette sit in the middle of the bed, then she would gently lay Melissa in Bernadette's lap, which Bernadette loved and enjoyed very much. During those three months, our life was delightful since nobody had to wake up early except me. The children's needs were taken care of, and dinner would be ready when I returned home from work.

However, such a lovely way of life was only temporary as Sylvia had to go back to work at the beginning of the fourth month, concluding her maternity leave. She was very hesitant to go back to work as we were very worried for both Bernadette and Melissa. At that time, Bernadette was only five years old, and Melissa was just four months old.

If we could only afford for Sylvia to be a stay-at-home mom, it would be heavenly as we both knew that the care of a mother is irreplaceable. Our hearts were again broken just by the thought of our very young daughters being left in the care of a babysitter who was a complete stranger to them. We knew that this would be the start of another cycle of hardships and sacrifices for all of us, very similar to what we had experienced when we first left Bernadette with the babysitter.

Even at the outset, we were already beginning to be burdened by a feeling of guilt. We were again torn apart by the conflicting choices. On the one hand, we were very worried about the quality of care for our very young daughters, and on the other hand, we wished to make a good living to provide our children with a brighter future.

Sylvia and I discussed this matter at great length, taking into consideration all our financial obligations. We both decided to go with the latter choice, which was a very hard decision.

Wanting to give Sylvia a little bit of comfort and peace of mind, I said to her, "We just have to keep our faith and continue to pray fervently every day that God will look after our young girls and that they will be protected from any harm, injury, and illness."

For the next few years, the daily routine started with everybody waking up early in the morning as we had to leave the house at 7:45. Sylvia would prepare breakfast for the girls, and I would start dressing them. We would alternate in feeding them while we also took turns getting ready. The night before, we usually prepared all the items that they would need for the following day.

We would drop off the girls at the babysitter's place around 8:15 a.m., and then we would rush off to take the trains to be at our respective jobs in New York City by 9:00 a.m. After work, we would pick them up from the babysitter's house around 6:00 p.m., arriving at our house around 6:30 p.m.

The nighttime chores were pretty hectic, involving bathing the girls first thing. While Sylvia cooked dinner, I would be preparing the usual things needed for the following day, including several bottles of milk for Melissa. Most nights, even before Sylvia would have the dinner ready, Melissa and I would be sound asleep in the rocking chair with the empty bottle of milk still in my hand.

It was during late fall of 1978, when Melissa was almost two and a half years old, that she and I, along with my brother, went back to the Philippines to visit my ailing father. That was the first and last time he saw his granddaughter Melissa. It was nevertheless a joyful and memorable homecoming. Both my parents were very happy to see Melissa for the first time. My father passed away in March of 1980, at the age of eighty-four.

Back to our life in the United States, over the next five years, we built a deep and intense bond with our two little girls. Our love for them and our concern for their well-being was paramount in everything we did. Each day of hardship and sacrifice that we endured together brought us significantly closer as a family and heightened our reliance on and trust in God, who strengthens us.

Our girls' babysitter was an elderly Filipina woman who was also taking care of her two granddaughters. The older one was about the same age as Bernadette, and the younger one, who had a congenital anomaly, was several months older than our Melissa. The babysitter had been recommended to us by a friend. Everything seemed fine during the first few months.

But as the next few months passed by, we began to observe that there were times when the care given to our girls, particularly to Melissa, was not very satisfactory. There were a few instances when we noticed that Melissa's rear end had some very red rashes on it, an indication that her diapers were not being changed often enough.

There were also a few times when we observed that some bottles of milk for Melissa were still half full, a sign that the babysitter may have been so busy with her other household chores that she neglected to give Melissa her milk. These were some of the observations that, even though relatively insignificant in the scheme of things, always made us cry and left us feeling guiltier. Given that Bernadette was just a five-year-old, we could not expect her to look after her younger sister all the time. She was most likely just enjoying herself playing with the babysitter's older granddaughter.

We had to be very careful and tactful, however, about the way we addressed these observations with the babysitter, as it was very difficult to find a relatively trustworthy babysitter who would agree to take care of two young girls. We did not have a problem as far as Bernadette's care was concerned.

It was during September of 1977, when Bernadette was six years old and ready to start kindergarten, when we had to change the babysitting arrangement. Melissa would continue to stay with the same elderly babysitter, while Bernadette, after school, would stay with two teenage Filipina girls who went to the same parochial school. Melissa stayed with the same babysitter for almost five years, and Bernadette stayed with the two teenage girls for almost four years.

In the summer of 1981, when Melissa was almost five years old and Bernadette was ten years old, we all went back to the Philippines to visit my ailing mother. Despite her medical condition, she welcomed us with great big smiles. She even cooked my favorite meal of grilled catfish with tamarind sauce mixed with fish sauce.

Although Bernadette hardly recognized her "mama," my sister who had taken care of her for two and a half years, the two of them eventually showed some kind of connection and, later on, expressed some affection toward each other. Everyone was impressed to see Bernadette growing up really nice and pretty. A year later, in December of 1982, my mother passed away at the age of eighty.

CHAPTER 14

Life in the Suburbs

IN THE EARLY spring of 1982, Sylvia and I decided to sell our first house in Jersey City and subsequently bought a house in Parlin, a suburb of Sayreville, New Jersey. We moved to the suburbs primarily for three reasons: (1) to give our young girls a safer place to grow up and play outside with the neighborhood children, (2) to give them the opportunity to attend a good public school, and (3) to live in an affordable area.

A few months after the move, it seemed as though we had made the right decision as everybody seemed to be enjoying the new environment. Our girls were starting to make new friends within the neighborhood, and both of them took the same bus to school. In the meantime, Sylvia and I would regularly commute to work in New York City.

After almost eight years working for the same company, I was offered a new and better-paying job at another nonprofit state banking trade organization as an accounting manager. Despite all the hardships we were enduring and the sacrifices we were making, Sylvia and I were beginning to feel somewhat optimistic about the future of our two girls and that our perseverance, determination, and hard work, so we thought, were gradually being rewarded.

The gradual but steady upward movement at my workplace, I believed, was largely attributable to my diligent hard work and constant desire to learn. I took computer classes at night, attended numerous industry conferences and seminars, enrolled in a public speaking workshop, and obtained my certification in the dynamics of supervision. I also became an avid reader of business magazines and the leading financial newspapers.

I was indeed very grateful and very proud of my accomplishments so far, and I felt as though my assimilation as a productive member of US society served as a testament to my successful transformation from an immigrant to a bona fide American citizen. More importantly, however, I was also very grateful to the Almighty God for His many blessings and merciful guidance.

We were starting to feel financially stable as all our financial obligations were being handled in a timely manner with some funds set aside as savings. On occasion, we were still able to send some money to our respective families in the Philippines, including Bernadette's mama.

Folks back home expressed their happiness for us and, how proud they were of our accomplishments so far.

Our two girls, meanwhile, were attending the local grade school, Emma L. Arleth Elementary School in Parlin. Melissa was in kindergarten, while Bernadette was in fourth grade. After school, both of them would stay with a teenage girl whose house was just a block away from our house.

In May of 1983, Melissa celebrated her seventh birthday with her cousins, some of the neighborhood kids, and her school friends. Everybody enjoyed the party as there were lots of food, birthday cake, ice cream, and goody bags. There was also a watermelon-eating contest, in which the participants could not use their hands. The kids threw water balloons, played with the Hula-Hoop in the swimming pool, and engaged in fun games with prizes. There was an unending amount of laughter among the kids, which was truly enjoyable for us to watch.

CHAPTER 15

The Medical Diagnosis

A FEW WEEKS before her birthday, Sylvia and I already had been very concerned about Melissa's health condition. She had lost a significant amount of weight, and she had an on-and-off fever. We took her to a local pediatrician in Parlin, who ordered blood work. She informed us that the result of the blood work was fine.

Since the on-and-off fever continued, on July 13, 1983, we decided to take Melissa to her former pediatrician in Bayonne for a second opinion. He immediately checked her vitals, and then he strongly recommended that a comprehensive blood test be done right away. He told us to take Melissa to the nearby Bayonne Hospital immediately. Meanwhile, we left Bernadette with the babysitter.

A Filipina doctor at the hospital told us to go into the waiting room as the blood test could take awhile. After waiting for about thirty minutes, which at the moment seemed more like an eternity, the hematology/oncology physician called us into her office and told us to sit down. Sylvia and I looked at each other with great concern as we could somehow sense that something was terribly wrong.

The doctor said, "I am very sorry, but I have some very bad news to tell you." Sylvia and I again looked at each other with great sadness and heaviness of heart. "The blood test revealed that the count on Melissa's white blood cells is abnormally very high, which is an indication that she has leukemia."

Upon hearing the word *leukemia*, Sylvia and I started to cry uncontrollably. At that moment, we felt as though the weight of the whole world had just collapsed on our shoulders. We were devastated and felt completely numb. I personally felt as if my heart had stopped beating for a few seconds. The tremendous emotional pain seemed to have penetrated even to my bones. I felt as though every fiber of my being had been terribly shaken.

The doctor finished up by saying, "Because Melissa has a very serious form of blood disorder known as acute lymphocytic leukemia, or ALL, we are sending her right away by ambulance to the Children's Hospital of New Jersey in Newark for immediate specialized treatment. Again, I am very sorry."

We just sat there motionless, unable even to say a word. All we could do was cry. It was an unexplainable feeling, but I thought I heard my soul crying, too.

Melissa looked at us with tears in her eyes, very concerned, confused, and afraid. Sylvia and I both lovingly hugged her while crying together and told her that we would stay with her all the time at the hospital during her treatment.

While we were hugging her, with tears rolling down her cheeks, Melissa turned to her mom. Her first words were, "Why me, Mommy? Why me?"

Before we could even think of what to say, we found ourselves once again crying uncontrollably, our emotions unrestrained. We felt as if our guts had been turned upside down. We did not know what to say, or what to think, or what to expect, or whom to turn to. In the silence of my heart, I found myself asking, *Where is God?*

At that very moment when mixed emotions were running high, we truly felt helpless and alone. After regaining a bit of composure, Sylvia found the courage to respond. She said, "I don't know, Melissa. I don't know." We truly did not know why these things happened. Nobody would ever know why except our great Lord and Creator.

After about half an hour had passed, an ambulance arrived. The

EMTs immediately put Melissa in a gurney and rushed to where the ambulance was parked, just outside the emergency main door, while Sylvia and I walked fast, trying to follow them. Melissa was strapped in a small bed inside the ambulance, and Sylvia was sitting close beside her. I followed the ambulance in my car.

At a close distance, although my eyes were focused on Melissa, I observed that the inside of the ambulance seemed very crowded with two emergency personnel busily attending to Melissa with a couple of IV machines and oxygen tanks stored off to the side. The ambulance was moving very fast, swerving left and right with its siren blaring and its colorful lights swirling around. I could see Sylvia holding Melissa's hands tightly. Both of them were crying.

I managed to stay close to the ambulance while occasionally wiping my tears. At that moment, I found myself silently praying that God would give us enough strength and courage during this very critical time in our life. I felt like I wanted to shout at the top of my lungs, but no words would come out.

After about forty-five minutes of hectic driving, we finally arrived at the hospital. Upon entering the main door to the hematology/oncology department, we observed that a team of doctors and nurses were already waiting for us.

In a matter of minutes, Melissa was already in her hospital gown and on her bed with both arms hooked up to IVs for medication. Meanwhile, Dr. Thomas Walters, the head of the department, told us to follow him to his office along with his team of physicians, including his colleague, Dr. Beverly Ryan.

Dr. Walters said, "Mr. and Mrs. Gabriel, I want to inform you of the different protocols and regimens that we are considering for the initial treatment of Melissa, including cranial radiation. These protocols are very similar to the ones currently being used by the Sloan Kettering Hospital in New York City."

Dr. Ryan added, "The first four to five months of treatment will be pretty aggressive, and some side effects are expected."

The gravity of the situation had not even sunk in, yet initial treatment already started. Listening to the doctors telling us about all the different protocols, regimens, and medical terms, which were all new to us, Sylvia and I both felt a tremendous amount of anxiety. It was quite overwhelming. It also seemed to me that events were moving so fast that we couldn't even think anymore, so we just sat there holding Melissa's hands with tears in our eyes.

At that very moment, I wished that I was able to lean to my parents for comfort and emotional support. Since they had passed away already, I felt like we didn't have anyone to turn to. I thought the only thing that was holding us together was our trust in God. My faith reminded me that He is the only one with the power to heal the wounds of my soul.

When all the medical people had left and only Melissa, Sylvia, and I remained in the room, we again found ourselves weeping very hard. As I looked at Sylvia, whose face and eyes were very red from crying, I felt a strong urge to tell her and Melissa that we should not lose hope and that we should continue to pray, even in the silence of our hearts, for God's guidance and mercy.

As the medication was beginning to take effect, Melissa started to feel sleepy. Before she went to sleep, and while Sylvia was hugging her, she repeated the question she asked her mom earlier: "Why me, Mommy? Why me?"

Sylvia's response was the same as before: "We don't know, Melissa. We just don't know." Her response made our hearts sink again. At that very moment of great sadness, with overwhelming anxiety gripping my mind and heart, all I could do was stare blankly at Melissa's face as she held her mom's hands. Melissa finally went to sleep with tears still in her eyes.

As it was almost 4:00 in the afternoon, I told Sylvia while Melissa was sleeping that I should head back home to pick up Bernadette from the babysitter. After dinner, Bernadette and I gathered clothes and other things needed by Sylvia and Melissa during their stay in the hospital. We also picked up some dinner for them on our way back.

On the way to the hospital, I told Bernadette about Melissa's diagnosis and said that the aggressive treatment would require Mom and Melissa to stay at the hospital for at least the next three months. Bernadette, who was only twelve years old at the time, did not say much. Even though she was not old enough to comprehend the gravity of the situation, I could sense that she was trying very hard to hold back her emotions.

During the entire treatment period, when our attention was focused on Melissa, we never heard a single complaint from Bernadette. She quietly did her daily schoolwork by herself and voluntarily helped in every little way she could by washing the dishes, making her bed, preparing the things that Melissa needed, and gathering the toys Melissa wanted. We could sense that Bernadette was very aware of our emotional anxiety, and we also knew that she tried her best not to cause trouble.

Since one of us had to be with Melissa during the initial period of intense treatment in the hospital, we had requested our respective employers to accommodate us with a special work arrangement for about three months, which they so understandingly granted us. The arrangement involved that I work three days a week and stay with Melissa in the hospital two days a week. Sylvia worked two days a week and stayed with Melissa in the hospital three days each week during her treatments. That arrangement also allowed for one of us to be with Bernadette after school hours and on weekends, which was a great relief. We also felt so grateful that our respective employers had afforded us that special work arrangement. However, there were some days when Sylvia had to take some of her work to the hospital in order to meet some month-end deadlines.

CHAPTER 16

The Chemotherapy Treatment

DURING THE FIRST four months of aggressive treatment, the initial protocol consisted of both chemotherapy and cranial radiation. Since Melissa's arms were hooked up to IVs for continued medication, she had to be transported by wheelchair to the radiation room.

We had observed that there were other patients about the same age as Melissa who were undergoing radiation treatment. On the first day of treatment, the department director explained to us the importance of cranial radiation, "This radiation treatment will prevent the leukemic cells from spreading into the brain, which, if that happens, is a grave complication of the disease. This treatment, in most cases, will have side effects. One likely side effect is that Melissa will lose her hair, but it will grow back again." Upon hearing that comment, Melissa looked very sad. Sylvia and I were holding back the tears.

The doctor proceeded to take out two markers from his desk, one red and the other orange. He asked Melissa, "Which color do you want me to use for drawing a line on your face?"

Melissa responded, "I like the red." He explained that the line would serve as guide for the technician to follow so that he could make the necessary adjustment and focus the machine to target only the parts of the head that needed treatment. He continued to gently mark a red line around Melissa's face.

As the doctors had warned that there would be some side effects from the aggressive chemotherapy and the cranial radiation, Melissa did experience occasional discomfort and pain in some parts of her body. Her hair would also fall out a few times during the course of the treatment. Every time Melissa heard of the hair loss side effect, she became silent with the sadness on her face easily discernible.

The doctors also emphasized that the initial regimen of experimental medicines would be very aggressive in order to stabilize Melissa's condition and to control the growth of the leukemic cells. They also informed us that the prevailing survival rate for ALL was 70 to 75 percent, which gave us comfort and some degree of hope and optimism.

The protocol required that Melissa undergo an intense six weeks of treatment at the hospital. Depending on the results, the doctors might then allow her to go home, at which time the treatment could be tapered off to three times a week starting with the seventh week and perhaps two times a week thereafter.

It was during the third week of treatment that an unusual side effect occurred. Melissa developed shingles on some parts of her chest and back, which, according to her, were annoyingly itchy and painful. She felt extremely uncomfortable. Her constant cries broke our hearts, and we found ourselves sobbing hard again.

At one particular moment when the three of us were crying, I suddenly remembered the advice of my mother. Her exact words were, "Son, when things are not going well for you and you feel like crying, that's the time you should pray intensely because prayer is very effective when it comes from the heart."

The nurse increasingly applied some medication to Melissa's skin to alleviate the pain and itchiness. While they were treating the skin problem, Melissa couldn't lie down. Most of the time she would sleep sitting on a chair with one arm hooked up to the IVs for continuous medication. Sylvia and I would insert a small pillow to support her head when she was about to fall asleep.

The following week, it was my turn to be with Melissa at the hospital. After dropping off Bernadette at the babysitter's house, I drove directly to the hospital, getting there around 7:30 a.m. with a home-cooked breakfast for Melissa.

Sylvia was dressed and ready to go to work when I arrived. She hugged Melissa and said goodbye to her. I saw Sylvia wiping her tears as she was leaving the room. It also brought tears to my eyes. I immediately wiped them away as I did not want Melissa to see me crying. I wanted to project the image of a strong father figure to her.

Melissa and I started the day watching her favorite morning cartoons on TV. I asked her if she wanted me to feed her because her left arm was hooked up to an IV.

She replied, "Papa, just cut the hash brown and sausage in small pieces, and I'll be able to eat by myself. That way, you can read the papers while I eat and watch cartoons."

I said, "Okay, I'll do that."

After Melissa finished her breakfast, I went to the playroom to get some crayons, writing pads, puzzle games, playing cards, and some children's books, which I carried in a big plastic container. I also got a Rubik's Cube and some Play Doh. I knew Melissa loved to draw. She was very good at color coordinating the pictures she created.

As I was entering her room carrying the big container, I saw a big smile on her face. I said to her, "We're going to have lots of fun today."

She said, "Yup."

We spent most of the morning playing different games and occasionally watching cartoons together. I thought she had lots of fun as her laughter could be heard at times by the nurses stationed outside the hallway, about three rooms away. We only stopped playing if Melissa needed help to go to the bathroom, if she wanted to rest, or if the nurse needed to check her vitals and replenish her medication.

I tried very hard to cheer Melissa up, to make her happy and comfortable even if just for a day. After lunch was served, she took an afternoon nap. When she woke up, I asked her if she wanted to play some more games.

She said to me, "Pa, I think I'll do some more drawing and coloring while watching TV, so you can rest and take a nap yourself." I told her I was fine and that I truly enjoyed playing with her.

As it was getting late in the afternoon and I was expecting Sylvia to arrive from work shortly to relieve me, I started gathering the things I needed to take back home. When I was just about done putting everything in a plastic bag, Melissa turned to me and said, "Papa, I hope I did not give you a hard time today."

Upon hearing what she had just said, I tried hard to control my feelings. I had promised myself not to cry, particularly around Melissa, but now my emotions overwhelmed me. I couldn't hold it in anymore.

After regaining my composure, I said to her, "Lis, you should not worry about me. You are the one who is going through a lot of hardships, pain, and discomfort."

She said, "I'm okay, Papa. I'm okay."

That was the first time I personally witnessed her incredible kindness, which I learned later on would be just one of several instances of her extraordinary compassion. Even at a very young age, she was highly attuned to our feelings and had learned to sense our every mood, which was largely affected by the ongoing stress and anxiety. I truly believe that her life-threatening illness contributed to her ability to think more maturely than the average seven-year-old.

During the beginning of the fourth week of treatment, when Melissa first experienced losing her hair, she was very sad and terribly upset. She cried long and hard.

She found herself repeating the same question she previously had asked her mom, saying, "Why me, Mommy? Why me? It's not fair that I have to suffer like this, when my friends and classmates are enjoying their lives."

Every time she asked that question, Sylvia and I found ourselves weeping uncontrollably. It was extremely difficult for us to come up with the right answer since there was none.

In my effort to somewhat console my daughter, I responded by saying, "Lis, we really don't know the reasons why. Even the doctors don't know the cause of your illness." Sylvia held Melissa's hands while wiping away her tears.

At the end of the fifth week of treatment, Melissa's condition began to stabilize, and her white blood cell count decreased to a normal level. The doctors informed us that, most likely, we could go home that weekend. Upon hearing such good news, we were all overwhelmed by the joyful excitement of finally being able to go home. Even Melissa had a happy smile on her face.

We all sighed a big sigh of relief and, at the same time, experienced heartfelt gratitude for the very positive news. The doctors informed us, however, that we needed to bring Melissa back to the hospital every other day for a checkup and treatment, which would last for about six months. The treatment schedule would be reduced to once a week for the six months after that. Such a positive development was welcomed with guarded optimism by all of us.

However, in between those periods of treatment, Melissa experienced several very painful side effects while at the hospital and at home. The treatment combination of chemotherapy and radiation was almost as dreadful as the disease. Several of the medicines being prescribed were part of the experimental protocol, the side effects of which were also somewhat new to the doctors.

As I recall, a chemo medicine called prednisone had several side effects, such as fever, chills, sore throat, coughing, puffy face, and a hungry feeling. Methotrexate, another strong chemo medicine, caused painful mouth ulcers, nausea, diarrhea, some skin reactions, and other problems.

Sylvia was taught by the nurses how to inject one of the medications into Melissa's thigh while she was home. That was quite a traumatic experience in the beginning. The first two or three times, Sylvia's hand started to shake, and she told me to hold Melissa's thigh steady. The needle was relatively long, and at the initial thrust of the needle, Melissa would yell and cry, begging us to stop, as it was very painful. We all, however, eventually adapted to the process, which became less and less traumatic for everybody.

There was a time when Melissa completely lost her appetite, leading to significant weight loss. Another time, her face became puffy and her stomach bloated. She developed shingles, experienced jaw pain, lost her hair a few more times, threw up right after eating, woke up in the middle of the night very hungry, and had fevers with blisters several times.

For a young girl, I think the hair loss was the hardest of the side effects for Melissa to accept. Sylvia bought her a dozen bandannas in various colors and styles, which she used to cover her head whenever she went out of the house. She would match the color of the bandanna with her outfit. She became very adept at using the bandannas in a number of ways that suited her style.

The second time Melissa lost her hair, it grew back wavy and curly, which was very different from her naturally straight hair. She liked it very much and asked her mom not to cut it, saying that she wanted to see curly locks grow down to her shoulders.

However, at one point when Sylvia was helping Melissa take a shower and combing her long and curly hair, Sylvia noticed that some of the hair remained in the comb, which was a sign that it was starting to fall out again. Sylvia was not able to control her emotions; tears started to flow down her face.

When Melissa saw her mom crying, she calmly told her, "Don't worry, Mommy, it will grow back again." On several occasions, Melissa had demonstrated an uncanny ability to stay calm and courageous whenever she sensed that we had been overcome with anxiety.

I recall an instance when Melissa woke me up around 2:00 in the morning and asked me to heat up some food as she was very hungry, a side effect of the medication. She knew that I usually woke up around 5:00 a.m. to start preparing for my long commute to work in New York City. She said to me, "Papa, just heat up the food. I'll eat in the kitchen. You can go back to sleep on the couch. I'll wake you up when I'm done eating."

I said, "Okay, I'll do that." In my mind, that was another example of how considerate and kind she was.

Bernadette, who was only twelve years old at that time, had also had her share of hardships and sacrifices. During the entire period of Melissa's intense treatment, Bernadette would usually be at the babysitter's house after school. She did her homework there while waiting for either her mom or me to pick her up around 6:30 p.m. She learned early on to be self-sufficient, and like Melissa, she also demonstrated mature perspectives brought forth by the very difficult situation we were all faced with.

There were several instances where we had to rush Melissa to the hospital in the middle of the night because she had a very high fever. We also had to wake Bernadette up since we did not want her to stay alone in the house. She would continue sleeping in the car and on a chair in the hospital emergency room.

Meanwhile, the daily physical and emotional stress brought forth by the tremendous responsibility of caring for a gravely ill child while taking care of other family needs, the household chores, and our work obligations was beginning to take its toll on all of us. Arguments would flare up sometimes. Occasionally Sylvia and I would exchange heated words, and our tempers would sometimes surface for no reason at all. The daily pressures undoubtedly were putting our marriage to the test.

There were times when I felt that the burden was unbearable. At times I found myself asking God when all this would end. But throughout the most difficult and critical times of our life, in some mysterious way, we each gradually learned how to control our emotions, adjusted to each other's feelings and temperament, persevered tremendously, prayed together passionately, and stuck together as a family.

In retrospect, considering what we went through as a family and having closely witnessed how Melissa courageously and righteously lived her fulfilled life, we eventually realized how blessed we were for having a child like Melissa.

CHAPTER 17

Lasting New Relationships

DURING MELISSA'S ENTIRE treatment period, we were blessed to have met some genuinely kind and very nice people. Since Sylvia was not comfortable enough to drive Melissa to the hospital by herself, we requested some assistance from the American Cancer Society. Merth was one of the regular volunteer drivers, and she was very compassionate. She happened to be a retired executive from a telecommunications company.

Merth volunteered to drive children with cancer to and from the different hospitals, and we very much appreciated her genuine concern for Melissa. She would always have some nice surprises for Melissa at her birthdays and during the holidays, which always brought a smile to Melissa's face. I recall one of Merth's touching comments to us: "Rod and Sylvia, I don't know what it is, but I always feel happy inside whenever I see Melissa smiling." She eventually became a close family friend.

Melissa's first grade teacher, named Miss Diana Lynch, who was passionate about education, volunteered to provide continuous homeschooling to her during the treatment period. Miss Lynch regularly came to our house every afternoon for almost four years to teach Melissa on a one-to-one basis, except on the days when Melissa felt good enough to attend school. Miss Lynch also became a dear family friend.

A former colleague of mine, named Walter Mullins, was a kind and respectable gentleman, whose support I truly appreciated. When he learned about Melissa's illness, he immediately offered to help me in whatever way he could.

I vividly remember his exact words: "Rod, please let me know if there is something that I can do to help you and your family—anything at all."

When he found out that Melissa loved working with different arts and crafts, drawing and writing poems, he gifted her with two very nice wooden briefcases full of various colorful art supplies. Melissa wrote a beautiful thank-you note to Walter:

Dear Mr. Mullins and Family,

Thank you very much for the art supplies. I sure will enjoy them for a long time. It was very nice of you to do such a kind thing. I may not know you very well, but I sure know that you're someone who makes this world and my life a whole lot better.

The world could use a whole lot of your kind of people. I shall treasure your love for me and my family forever. I hope to see you and your family soon.

Love,
Melissa

Melissa also developed a very close friendship with one of the cancer patients named Michelle Scotto, who was a year older than she.

There were times when their hospital rooms were next to each other. They often spent time together in the playroom, and they truly enjoyed playing together along with the other leukemia patients.

Melissa wrote a special poem about her friendship with Michelle, a reflection of their close companionship:

A Special Bond, Friendship

We have a very special bond.
Nobody or nothing can break this bond.
It's a combination of love, trust, caring,
hope, and sharing.
It gives you a feeling of protection.
Our spirits, thoughts, and feelings
Are always together.
This very special bond is our friendship!

In the summer of 1985, the Valerie Fund for Children, a nonprofit organization whose primary mission is to help children afflicted with cancer, sponsored a summer camp for young cancer patients. Melissa attended the camp for a week with Michelle and with other patients from different hospitals. Several doctors and nurses also stayed with the group.

Melissa told us later on that she really had a good time doing lots of activities with the other children, such as swimming, horseback riding, fishing, bicycling, and kayaking. They were also taught by the nurses how to be independent for one week, with the nurses showing them how to make their beds, fold their own clothes, attend to their personal chores, and get along nicely with other kids.

At nighttime, they would sing together while gathered around a bonfire. One night, Melissa said that they really had a fun time with the nurses who helped the girls color and spike their hair with gel. They also put some temporary tattoos on the kids' arms and necks, which was very amusing.

CHAPTER 18

Remissions and Relapses

AFTER ALMOST TWO years of treatment, in late summer of 1985, the doctors informed us of the really great news that Melissa's recent checkup revealed no presence of leukemic cells, which meant she was in her first remission. We all shed many tears of immense joy and overwhelming relief and felt very grateful to God for the positive development. The doctors also told us that they would only be seeing Melissa for checkups and maintenance treatment on a quarterly basis.

After hearing such good news, we decided that Sylvia should quit her job immediately so that she could devote all her time to care for Melissa with the hope of preserving her remission status. Melissa felt as though she was the happiest nine-year-old on earth. There was no more painful treatment or dreadful side effects, and her mom would be with her all the time.

During this period, Melissa was able to attend school regularly, play outside with friends and neighbors, eat anything she liked, go to the movies, and attend birthday parties, practically everything that a normal nine-year-old would do.

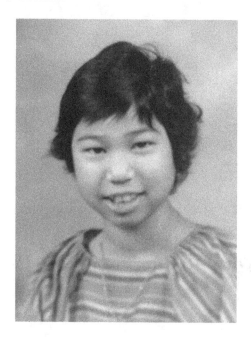

We had the most memorable and happiest Christmas celebration that year, which was attended by lots of relatives, friends, and neighbors. We had a group prayer before dinner, and everybody was emotional. We thanked God very much that Melissa was with us and in remission.

Melissa started her diary when she was nine years old. Following are a few of her early entries and personal reflections:

December 6, 1985

Today is the first day of snow. It is great. It went about one inch high. I started to make a few footprints in the snow. I hope it will get higher, like up to my knees.

Sincerely yours,
Melissa

December 7, 1985

Today I wished it was Christmas or that we would get our encyclopedia. I've been waiting so long. This morning my mom is trying to play the song that the piano plays.

Someday I want to write about my illness, about my experience, and about my relapse.

In mid-January of 1986, we were informed by the doctors that the count of Melissa's white blood cells had gone up significantly, which indicated that she was having a relapse. Everybody was very upset. Once again, we found ourselves crying very hard.

Melissa reflects on her first relapse:

January 13, 1986

Today I went to the Newark hospital for a blood test. But [my count] was too high. It was twenty-two thousand, which is above normal. They did a bone marrow test on me and found some leukemic cells. That means I'm out of remission. I stayed in the hospital for three days. Everyone is upset.

God, why me?

I first got leukemia on July 13, 1983.

Such a setback meant that Melissa had to undergo another session of chemotherapy, this time a more aggressive treatment, with its unforgiving side effects. Our family had to follow the same very difficult, hectic, and anxiety-filled treatment schedule again, which I personally felt to be a gut-wrenching emotional roller-coaster experience. Everybody's feelings and moods swung like a pendulum depending on Melissa's condition.

Once every three months, Melissa had to undergo the extremely painful bone marrow checkup, also called a spinal tap, which required that the doctor insert a very long needle in between the last two vertebrae at her lower back. The procedure was necessary to get a sample tissue of the marrow to determine the condition of the marrow cells. Even with the administration of a local anesthesia, the pain was so unbearable that I could still hear Melissa's loud cries even at a great distance.

Meanwhile, there was another memorable day in late December of 1986, when I witnessed yet another demonstration of Melissa's incredible kindness. The heavy snowstorm on that particular winter day caused major traffic, which delayed my commute home by several hours.

When I got to the commuters' parking lot, I found out that my car was almost buried in snow. The situation was aggravated by the fact that I'd forgotten to bring a shovel and a hat that day. Since the only tool I had in the car was a handheld ice scraper, typically used to scrape ice off the windows, it took me an extra thirty minutes just to clear the snow off my entire car. I finally reached home around 9:30 p.m., which was three hours later than my usual arrival time. I was completely soaked and very hungry.

Just as soon as I reached the front door of our house, Melissa was already waiting for me with a towel in her hand, which she used to start drying my hair. Then she said to me, "Papa, give me your briefcase. After you change your clothes, just lie down in your bed to rest, and I'll feed you."

After hearing that, it almost brought tears to my eyes as I could feel her genuine concern for me. After regaining some composure, my response to her was, "Lis, thank you very much, but I think I still have the energy to eat by myself in the kitchen. Just help your mom set the table for me."

Meanwhile, during the five years of chemo treatment, Bernadette was always very supportive of her younger sister. Whenever Melissa felt better and was off her medications, Bernadette made sure to be around her at all times. It was during those hard and long years that we observed a close bond growing between our two young girls.

We knew that Bernadette sacrificed a lot, too, as she selflessly spent most of her teenage years playing with Melissa. On many occasions, they would sing together as a duet. They tape-recorded a few songs, imitating Madonna and Cyndi Lauper, their favorite pop singers at that time.

It was in early January of 1987 when we found out the good news that Sylvia was pregnant. She was due in early November, right before she would turn forty-two years old. The pregnancy was neither planned nor expected since Sylvia never experienced the usual morning sickness.

Back then, having a baby after forty was pretty uncommon. This was a lot to take in as we were in the midst of caring for a critically ill daughter. However, Sylvia and I both believed that a new addition to our family was a gift from God that we had to accept wholeheartedly.

January 9, 1987

Today my mommy said that she is pregnant. We don't know if it's a boy or girl or if he

*or she is normal or not. I hope he or she
is normal.*

*I'm happy, but I guess I have to share [the]
attention [I get] from Mom and Papa. At
least I'll have someone to play with and
boss around. I've got a nickname, "Snooty."
Well, my mom is going for the test in May.*

During the first half of 1987, Melissa was able to enjoy going back
to school, bike around with some friends, and go shopping at the mall.
She felt blessed to have been given some time off from chemo treatment,
and she was truly happy, living like a normal eleven-year-old.

June 26, 1987

*Today we found out the sex of the baby my
mom is going to have. It is a normal baby
boy. We are so happy. We even called Papa
at his office to tell him. The baby will be
named Rod Robert.*

But those precious moments were rather short-lived because in late
August, Melissa had her second relapse. She was devastated, feeling
as though life was very unfair. She dreaded having to resume chemo
treatment and experience its horrible side effects, such as losing hair
again and undergoing the painful bone marrow aspirations. She
absolutely did not look forward to staying in the hospital for weeks and
missing school again.

August 24, 1987

Dear Diary,

Today I feel like hating life because I found out that I had my second relapse. It's not fair that I have to start all over. Why can't other children get it [instead of] me? Did I do something so bad that I got this?

It all started with aches in my bones. Then when I got to the hospital, they suspected it was blasts, [so they] did a bone marrow [test] and found some blasts.

It's not fair!

As she had done during the first relapse, Melissa cried a great deal. There were several nights when she'd fall asleep with tears running down her cheeks. While gently wiping her tears away, Sylvia and I would also find ourselves quietly sobbing, holding Melissa's hands.

August 26, 1987

Dear Diary,

Today I start my chemotherapy to put me in remission again. It is the hardest part because they use larger doses of medicine, [which] could make me sick and [cause] my hair [to] fall out. Also, I will miss my first two weeks of school, [which] I was looking forward to ..., so I have to get a tutor.

I was supposed to pick up my schedule, but today I was admitted to the hospital to start the chemo. I stayed overnight while throwing up every hour. It was horrible. I couldn't sleep a wink or eat.

Yours truly,
Melissa

In between chemo treatments, whenever she felt strong enough, Melissa very much enjoyed going to school to share a few laughs with her classmates. She also enjoyed doing her favorite activities like drawing, coloring, swimming, and biking around with other neighborhood kids.

September 22, 1987

Dear Diary,

Today I just found out I'm back in remission from my second relapse. I'm so happy. I just prayed the rosary to thank Jesus. I feel great.

But now I just pray that I survive my new treatment.

October 27, 1987

Dear Diary,

Today I started tutoring with Miss Lynch [again]. It was great, but I've got a lot of homework. I prayed the rosary today.

CHAPTER 19

The Birth of Our Son

IN EARLY NOVEMBER 1987, our third child, a baby boy, was born. We nicknamed him Bobby.

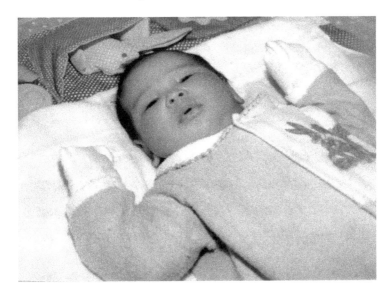

Early November 1987

Dear Diary,

Today is my mom's induction, but when they gave her the medicine, the baby's pulse got lower, so they had to open her up. Robert was born in Perth Amboy Hospital. [The] doctor [was] Revilla Zapanta. Time born: 1:14 p.m. Weight: 8 lb., 7 oz. Length: 21.5 inches. He is so cute. I even got to touch him. The first time I saw him was [at] 1:32 p.m. My mom is okay also. I will pray for both of them. They can't come home until Monday or Tuesday.

Melissa was very happy and excited to have a baby brother.

November 8, 1987

Dear Diary,

Today Bobby had his circumcision done. I [can tell it] hurts when he makes pee because he cries. He also smiled at me for the first time. I will pray for him to be strong.

November 9, 1987

Dear Diary,

Today Bobby and Mommy are coming home. He is so adorable. I carried him in the car. I decorated the house. I'm so excited.

November 21, 1987

Dear Diary,

Today was the first time Bobby saw [a] television. We're having a ball with him. He's three weeks old.

November 25, 1987

Dear Diary,

Today was Bobby's first doctor's appointment. His doctor is Dr. Barakat. She's very nice and good. She even knows Dr. Walters, my doctor. She made funny remarks about him.

December 5, 1987

Dear Diary,

Today was Bobby's first bath in tub. He was crying of course. We all had to help him because it was hot. He was so cute.

Also, we put up our Christmas tree with candy, tinsel, lights, [and] decorations. It was fun. I put my gifts [under it] already.

December 21, 1987

Dear Diary,

Today Bobby started to make sounds. Some of them sounded like ma, ya, and no. He's so chubby and cute.

December 31, 1987

Dear Diary,

Today was Bobby's first New Year's Eve with us. It went pretty fast, but I bet this year is going to be better. We [banged] pots [together], jingled coins in our hands, and

drank wine. I got a dizzy spell from it.
Happy New Year!

Yours truly,
Melissa

However, by mid-January 1988, Melissa had her third relapse.

January 13, 1988

Dear Diary,

It happened again. My third relapse. Nice
new year, huh? It's just not fair. I guess
I have to live [with] it.

I hope this is it!

Despite the daily struggles, Melissa carried on with her life. She continued her homeschooling with Miss Lynch, played with her sister and baby brother, and joined the occasional get-togethers with our relatives. She even helped her mommy take care of her brother while going through her chemo treatment despite its adverse effects.

Prior to Bobby's birth, Melissa would always sleep with Sylvia in our bedroom. She felt very comfortable and slept soundly while snuggled in with her mom. However, she agreed gladly and without hesitation when Sylvia asked her if she could sleep in her own room so Sylvia can stay with Bobby throughout the night.

Melissa asked me afterward, "Papa, is it okay with you if you stay with me and sleep in my room?"

I immediately responded, "Of course, Lis. I'd be happy to."

Over the next few months, I slept on the floor next to Melissa's bed. On several occasions, she asked me to hold her hand, which, I think, provided her with some feeling of comfort and security as she would quickly fall asleep while still holding my hand.

Even when Bobby was just a few months old, there were a few times when we had to take him with us to the hospital for Melissa's treatments and regular checkups.

It was in late January of 1988 when we decided to call Sylvia's mother in the Philippines to ask her if she would consider coming to the US and help us if we were able to secure a tourist visa for her. After a few weeks, and after consulting with her husband, she agreed to our request.

With the assistance of a local congressman, we were able to obtain a tourist visa for Sylvia's mother within a relatively short period of time. She arrived in the United States on April 12, 1988. She was a great help to my family as she handled most of the household chores, such as cooking and taking care of Bobby whenever we were at the hospital with Melissa.

However, in early June of that year, Dr. Ryan informed us of the incredibly sad news that Melissa's body was no longer responding positively to the new experimental protocol and that Melissa would continue to have leukemic cells in her system. We again felt very numb. For a moment, we were completely speechless. We just found ourselves crying hysterically.

Dr. Ryan said, "The last resort will be a bone marrow transplant. You can have all your family members do a blood test to find out if there is a match for a potential donor. The transplant can only be done if Melissa is in remission."

Dr. Ryan also mentioned that she would be leaving the hospital within the month and that Dr. Nepo, another oncology and hematology specialist, would be replacing her. We expressed our gratitude to her and wished her good luck, telling her that we would miss her. With enormous sadness in her voice, she said, "I'll miss you too. I'm very sorry about your daughter Melissa."

On the way home from the hospital, we were very quiet. Even though I knew that Melissa could sense that something was wrong, she did not say a word. From the rearview mirror, however, I could see a tremendous sadness in her face.

During the next few weeks, everybody in my immediate family went for a blood test. Afterwards, the tests revealed that our son, Bobby, who was just about four months old at that time, was a perfect match.

Sylvia and I talked about the situation, and we decided that if Melissa were to go back into remission, we would try the bone marrow transplant. We called Dr. Nepo and asked her if it would be okay if we informed Melissa about the possible transplant. She said that would be fine.

When we told Melissa about the plan, she started to cry. In a begging tone of voice, she said, "Mommy, Papa, please don't do it. Bobby is just a baby." She added, "I am willing to die so that my baby brother doesn't have to go through the pain."

Upon hearing her words, both Sylvia and I just broke down weeping. We lovingly hugged Melissa. In the silence of my heart, I said to myself, *Melissa is really very special.*

Melissa once again had shown how much she loved her family. She had just demonstrated the ultimate sign of true love and selflessness by willingly putting herself on the line for the sake of a loved one.

It took me awhile before I was able to collect myself. Once I had regained my composure, I said, "Lis, we don't have to worry about that now. Dr. Ryan told us that the transplant can only be done if you get back into remission."

Melissa's response was, "I still don't want to do it."

I just said, "Okay."

Unfortunately, the alternative plan for a bone marrow transplant was not pursued as Melissa had not returned to remission.

In late July of 1988, Dr. Nepo informed us of a program being sponsored by the Starlight Foundation that would grant the last wish of a critically ill child. Indicating that Melissa would qualify for that program, she asked us if our daughter had any such wish. Since we were not ready for any response, we asked Dr. Nepo to give us a couple of days to think about it.

The following day, Sylvia and I sat down with Melissa to discuss her wish. We asked her what she wanted to do or where she wanted to go. Her immediate response was, "Mommy, Papa, it's up to you. Wherever you want us to go, we will all go."

Quite touched by Melissa's response, we found ourselves crying again. Sylvia suggested a religious trip to Lourdes, France. The Lourdes grotto is a well-known holy place where the Virgin Mary, centuries ago, appeared before three young girls, including Saint Bernadette. Miraculous healings were known to have happened there.

Since everybody agreed that it was a very good idea, we immediately called Dr. Nepo to inform her of our family's decision to go to Lourdes, France.

CHAPTER 20

Religious Trip to Lourdes, France

IN SEPTEMBER OF 1988, the entire family, including my mother-in-law, left New Jersey to head to Lourdes, France, for a weeklong religious trip.

September 16, 1988

Dear Diary,

Today we are leaving for France at 3:00 p.m. Michael from the Starlight Foundation is having his chauffer pick us up in his stretch limousine. It's going to be my first time riding in a limo.

We're going to France for one week. We'll be back the twenty-fifth. We're going to Lourdes grotto. I'm so excited.

We're flying some unknown Catholic airline. But it's better than nothing. A doctor is going to be on the plane, too. So there's probably a bunch of sick people. The trip is about seven hours. The time difference is six hours from the USA. Our seats are 26C, Papa; 26D and 26E, me; 26F, Bobby; 26G, Mom; 26H, Ate ["older sister" in Tagalog]; and 26J, Lola ["Grandmother" in Tagalog].

When we arrived at the John F. Kennedy International Airport in New York, a representative from the Starlight Foundation welcomed us and told us to follow him to a waiting airplane. Once inside the plane, we found out that it was a chartered flight arranged for by the American Catholic Society in coordination with the Starlight Foundation. There were about two hundred critically ill children from across the nation who were going with us to Lourdes, along with their families and some medical doctors, some nurses, and a priest.

Our entire group stayed together in the same big hotel, which was within walking distance of a huge cathedral. The place was packed with people who had come from different countries. There were about seven masses every day, translated simultaneously into different languages.

Every night around 6:00, there was a long prayer procession led by a priest heading toward the cathedral. A lot of the sick children attended this daily activity with each of them holding a candle while praying and singing hymns. The procession was incredibly solemn and quite touching.

Some of the children were being wheeled in while lying on beds; some of them walked using walkers, crutches, or canes; and many of the others were escorted in wheelchairs, including Melissa. We witnessed the courage, faith, sacrifice, and determination of those children praying for a miraculous healing.

We also met some very nice people at Lourdes, including a family from Texas with their teenage son, Ronny, who was totally paralyzed from a devastating car accident. He could only communicate by pressing the buttons on a machine attached to his wheelchair. The boy's mother, Marie, was especially nice to Melissa, giving her a big, warm hug when we told her of Melissa's condition.

Upon learning of Ronny's condition, Melissa tried to make conversation with him through his machine. Even though Melissa was gravely ill herself, I could sense that she had an innate tendency to show some compassion toward those she felt were less fortunate than she. While at Lourdes, Melissa wrote a letter to Marie:

Dear Marie,

I'm really glad to have met you and your family. You are all very kind, loving, caring, special, and blessed people. The world needs more people like you. Today there are so many problems that bring pain and suffering in this imperfect world. Some people, or [at least those who are] healthy and normal, don't realize their gift of life and value it as much as the hurt, poor, and afflicted [do]. I guess until that gift God gave to you is taken away, you won't really realize its true value.

I've been fighting leukemia for five years now, and now the doctors have given up.

Today's modern medicine can't cure me, so that's why we're here in Lourdes, to ask the Blessed Mother to heal [me]. My family loves me dearly and won't let me go. It must be hard for you also. But it's so nice to always see you smiling because it makes me feel good, too.

God bless your family and you. I hope to see you or keep in touch. I'll miss you. Bye!

Love forever,
Melissa Gabriel

We also observed an instance of Melissa extending a helping hand to another disabled boy, a complete stranger, who had trouble walking. We found out that he and his mother had come all the way from the Philippines to participate in the pilgrimage. She told us that her son had an unusual disorder that hindered his growth, which explained his very short stature and more mature-looking face.

On the fourth day of the trip, Melissa decided to join the other kids in taking a quick dip in a tub that contained holy water originating from the natural spring behind the grotto. I touched the water; it was pretty cold.

Afterward, our group went to pray in front of the grotto, where the statue of the Virgin Mary was enshrined. We placed some candles beneath the statue. My entire family, Melissa in particular, enjoyed the overall solemn atmosphere at Lourdes.

September 25, 1988

Dear Diary,

Today is our resting day from our trip to France. We got home at 11:30 last night 'cause the limo that was supposed to pick us up wasn't there, also because our plane in Lourdes was delayed for four hours. But it was beautiful in France.

We met many nice people, did a lot of shopping for family and friends, ate splendid food, prayed, and attended most of the religious activities. One nice thing was [that] the shops and praying places were [within] walking distance from the hotel.

We also saw [a lot of] beautiful scenery like you've never seen before. The place gives you a special feeling. I want to go back very badly.

CHAPTER 21

Melissa's Last Days

ON SEPTEMBER 25, 1988, we made our trip back home to New Jersey. Melissa seemed very uncomfortable during the entire flight. On our second day back home, Melissa developed a fever and was complaining of some back pain. We immediately rushed her to the hospital, where the doctors found out that she had a bad case of pneumonia. Bernadette and Bobby had stayed at home with their grandmother.

From then on, Melissa's health condition continued to deteriorate. Her appetite was very poor, and despite being fed intravenously, her weight loss was significant. Her entire body was in constant pain. To alleviate the pain, the doctors ordered for her to be given morphine intermittently.

Melissa had lost her hair completely. She became very thin with breathing and feeding tubes connected to her nose and mouth, and her body looked very fragile. When I was by her side, I saw her pain through her occasional smiles. I was very much heartbroken, feeling completely helpless. Tears started to roll down my face at the sight of my daughter in such a horrible condition.

On the night of October 8, 1988, at around 11:00, while looking at Melissa with deep compassion, I suddenly felt a powerful urge to tell her what was in my heart. I remember vividly that last heart-to-heart talk with my Melissa.

With a shaky voice and a heavy heart, I said to her, "Lis, wherever you're going, someday I'd like to join you."

She immediately responded by saying, "Pretty soon, Papa. Pretty soon." She added, "And you know, Papa, Mommy, the only thing that is keeping me here on earth is your love for me."

Upon hearing what she had just said, Sylvia and I cried uncontrollably. I had observed, however, that Melissa was not crying and she appeared to be very calm. She said to us, "Mommy, Papa, do not cry. I'll be okay. And whenever I get a chance, I'll come and visit you."

As if an older and wiser person were counseling us for the last time, she said, "You, Papa, sometimes said things to Mommy that you should never have said."

My response to her was, "I'm very sorry, Lis, but sometimes, because I'm under a lot of pressure, I say things that I don't really mean."

Melissa turned toward her mom and said, "You, Mommy, always get mad, even at little things."

Sylvia, who was still crying and was overwhelmed with emotion, could only say, "I'm sorry, Lis. I'm really sorry."

Immediately thereafter, Melissa asked her mommy, "What time is it, Mom?" She asked the same question a few times as if she had an appointment to meet with someone or as if she had somewhere to go.

In early morning of the following day, October 9, 1988, at about 3:00, Melissa was gasping for her last breath as her heart rate was slowing down rapidly. The machine was making lots of beeping sounds. After a few seconds, however, we heard an emergency message from the loudspeaker: "Code Blue. Code Blue."

We then heard some commotion. The nurses and doctors ordered us to stay out of the room because the Code Blue team, as part of their normal protocol, was trying to resuscitate our daughter.

After a few minutes, Dr. Nepo came out of Melissa's room. In a very sad and soft voice, she said, "Rod, they are having a hard time resuscitating Melissa. Even if they are successful, Melissa will be like a vegetable. I suggest that you let her go and let her rest."

Upon hearing that, I think I might have just nodded my head while crying hysterically. It was so loud that the entire hospital staff must have heard it. Dr. Nepo hugged me tight and said, "I'm very sorry. Melissa has just left us."

While still crying in a loud and piercing way, I thought I had heard my soul crying too, for the second time. At that very moment, I also felt a piece of my heart leave with Melissa.

Afterward, I called my brother, who at that time lived in Jersey City, which was about thirty minutes away from the hospital. He told me that he would be with us in a few minutes and that he would drive me and Sylvia back home.

Just as soon as we reached our driveway, I noticed that Sylvia's mother had already opened the front door. Since everybody was so quiet, sad, and somber, Bernadette asked what had happened. I told her to have a seat with us on the couch.

Sylvia and I held Bernadette's hands. I said to her, "Your sister has just left us." Without saying a word, Bernadette fell to the floor, crying and rolling her body back and forth. We hugged her lovingly and helped her to get up. Bernadette was truly devastated just like us.

We were all greatly affected by the death of Melissa and will always feel that loss. But we also feel blessed that she was part of our lives and left a lasting impression on us. She is now our true guardian angel.

CHAPTER 22

Other Entries from Melissa's Diary

March 24, 1986

On Tuesday, the eighteenth of March 1986, I got my Broviac [catheter] because I didn't have any good veins. When I woke up, my neck felt sore. I couldn't move it.

On Thursday, the twentieth, I got out of the hospital. I thanked God because I [had been] in the hospital for three weeks.

April 2, 1986

Today I just want to tell you that Easter Sunday, March 30, 1986, I was admitted into the hospital and got out on April 6.

Rose Ann, my cousin, came to visit me.

Oh, I got the tape from my class back (fourth grade class). They all sound the same.

May 21, 1986

Today I want to tell you [that] a long time ago I watched a movie called Alex. It's a true story about a girl born with a disease that no one can cure. She was born with it and dies with it.

I look up to [the main character, Alex]. [I want to] be brave and to have hope [like her].

May 21, 1986

I want to tell you about Jose. He passed away. It all happened like this: He got the transplant, and everything was okay. Then he had an infection and fell into a coma. He never woke up. He's a fighter like Michelle and Alex.

September 2, 1986

Today is the last day of summer. I went to the clinic today. I heard Laela died, too. Her mom has different beliefs and tried [a] different treatment. Laela got worse.

[Laela] couldn't get back to remission. I will pray for her.

Thursday, December 11, 1986

Today around 2:30 p.m. it started to snow for the first time this year. I'm moving on December 20, 1986, to Sayreville, NJ. I will miss the house in Parlin. We lived here for four years and four months. This new house is a bilevel, has an in-ground pool with Tarzan swing and low diving board, [and] a lot of room still for [a] picnic area.

Friday, December 12, 1986

Today I just heard Justin died. I really miss him, although I didn't cry that much *because I was at the hospital. It hurts so much. He was only three years old and had neuroblastoma.*

Four people [have] left me already. It's not fair. I'm starting all over again with pain. He meant so much to me.

June 6, 1987

Today I'm going shopping with Carolyn, my best friend; her sister Grace; and Ate.

We're setting up for my friend's party for me. The people invited are friends from my school and neighbors from Parlin.

June 17, 1987

Today is my Moving Up ceremony (graduation) in Arleth School. I'm in fifth grade (year 1986–1987). My teacher is Mrs. Malik. Our music teacher who directed us is Mrs. Daniash. We sang "America the Beautiful," "The Star-Spangled Banner," and "God Bless the USA."

June 22, 1987

Today is our last day of school. This was my last year in Arleth School. I miss everyone. Christina and Joanna, my close friends, are moving to Florida.

I went to Jackie's birthday party. It was fun. I got her a pink purse. It was from 5:30 to 10:00, but I stayed until 9:00.

August 14, 1987

Today I had so much fun with my friend Melissa. It was the first time I really was independent and responsible for myself.

First, we biked, and then [we] came back to her house to swim. It was so funny 'cause I kept trying to get on the inflatable raft and kept on slipping. Then we dried off and walked to Krauser's to buy candy. We bought candy shoelaces, a Skor bar, and Cherry Crush soda. Then we played a game, "Waiting for Mom." I loved it.

September 3, 1987

I just found out my Tita ["Aunt" in Tagalog] Cora is going to give my mom a surprise baby shower. It will be for Bobby, of course, at 3:00 p.m. on Saturday at our house.

She will bring Tito ["Uncle" in Tagalog] Teddy's family, Tita Gaying, Tita Baby, Tita Letty, and others. I will also invite Marilyn from my hospital. She called Papa at his office. I can't wait.

September 11, 1987

Today I just found out Lola might be coming from the Philippines. Tito Teddy told us. She'll be coming before the baby comes. We will call tomorrow.

Sunday, September 20, 1987

Today is my parents' seventeenth wedding anniversary. It is the first ever celebrated in [the new house]. Ate and I cooked a good breakfast and put our homemade cards on the table. Mommy and Papa cried, but that's okay.

We also had to close our pool for the winter. It was our first time, but it's on Pa's and Ma's anniversary. I didn't like that.

But after we picked up Ate from Saint Bernadette's Church, we went to Carvel and bought a small ice cream cake and an ice cream cone for me. Then we had lunch and went to the Filipino store in Jersey City.

September 21, 1987

Today I just prayed the rosary. When I read this, I won't think much of it, but it is special. So I know when I take time out for the Lord. For He takes time out for you. I like to pray the rosary.

September 23, 1987

Today is the last day of summer season '87. Also, today, my new treatment is going to start. It is less aggressive than the induction period but more [aggressive] than the maintenance period. It will only be for two weeks, then I have two weeks' rest. But I have to go twice a week.

After two weeks' rest, I just have to go once a week for two years. The only thing is, I'm losing my hair again and it might take longer to grow back. And I don't know when I can go back to school. I really like school except for carrying the heavy books.

September 24, 1987

Today is our first vacation day of the year in school. We are celebrating Rosh Hashanah since it is a public school. At least I'm feeling good [enough] to do things. Ate is home, but Papa has work.

I also took time out to pray the rosary with Mom.

September 29, 1987

Today I just finished taking time out for Jesus in praying the rosary.

October 5, 1987

Today I just prayed the rosary. I took time out for Jesus.

Also, this weekend Papa finally put shelves in the bar, put plastic on the oriental rug, and rearranged the living room and barroom.

And this is my first week off from medicine [for] my second relapse. I have next week off, too. I hope Mom has the baby then. I can't wait!

October 6, 1987

Today I just prayed the rosary. I told Jesus that I would help carry the cross with Him.

Also, I started to play store/house after waiting for a week.

October 7, 1987

Today was my first time to pray the Glorious Mystery. It made me feel good. I feel secure when I pray the rosary.

October 8, 1987

Today I just finished praying the rosary. I feel secure now. I took time out for Jesus.

October 14, 1987

Today is only four days away [from when] my Lola and Tito Noel are coming. Well, we're not sure, because they didn't call, but Candy said Lola will come on October 18.

Also, I took time out for Jesus by praying the rosary. It was the Glorious Mystery today. I felt good afterward because I hadn't prayed in a long time. That was not good. I'll try not to do it again, because when I have low count, I can't go to church. This is the least I could do.

November 29, 1987

Today is my mom's forty-second birthday. We got her some gifts. I got her a Virgin Mary that sings "Ave Maria."

Ate got her an album for Bobby. His album is nicer than ours.

December 12, 1987

Today was the worst day of my life. I found out there was no Santa Claus. Also, our Toyota Camry got stolen. It had our Christmas gifts for everyone and my star, white jacket.

God, why does this happen to us! Is there a God?!

January 3, 1988

Dear Diary,

Today was when my father took my sister to learn how to drive. She [did] great for her first try. But whenever she pressed on the accelerator, Pa would be, like, going through the windshield. They used the Mercury Monarch (red).

January 29, 1988 (Flashback)

Today God talked to me through the radio. Well, I have the sore mouth. I feel awful because I'm taking prednisone.

The person on the radio said or explained why this was happening.

I felt better. I really believe there is a God.

April 12, 1988

Today my grandmother is here from the Philippines. She really came yesterday, but she stayed in Tito Teddy's house for the night. It was so hard to get her here. I just hope Lolo ["Grandfather" in Tagalog] will follow.

May 28, 1988

Yesterday was my twelfth birthday. I had a party with my friends. I just realized I was very lucky to reach twelve. But when I look at my friends with nice long hair, built bodies, and plenty to talk about [in regard to] a future, [I realize that] I don't have hair or a built body. I don't go to school. Mostly unlike other kids, I don't have a future. Most probably I'll be gone by my teens.

June 26, 1988

Today Ate got her first job at Laffin in South River. It's very close. She gets four dollars an hour. She works from 1:00 p.m. to 5:00 and is off weekends and holidays.

Laffin is a car dealer of Oldsmobile and Chevys. She can get a discount on her car. She is a receptionist who answers phones, types, and files.

July 16, 1988

Today is the first time Bobby went in the swimming pool. He's eight months. In the beginning he was scared, but he got used to it and started splashing.

July 29, 1988

Today is my last day of school, sixth grade. I was tutored by Miss Lynch. She is the one who always tutors me. I missed a lot of school; that's why I just got out. It's also my first year to take finals. They are very hard. I'll find out my score Monday, August 1, 1988.

August 24, 1988

Dear Diary,

Today is a very sad day. I went to the hospital, and they told me the leukemic cells were back. Although I didn't cry as much as the other three relapses I had, I still told myself that it wasn't fair.

I worked so hard to finish sixth grade until July, and now I'm not sure I want to go to seventh grade.

Every time I try to pick [up] the pieces I started [out] with and put them together, they shatter right before my eyes. But I know God always listens to my cry.

August 29, 1988

Dear Diary,

Today is the day I [have been] wait[ing] for all my life. Dr. Nepo called and said she saw no more blasts in my blood. Just after a week of treatment. It's a true miracle for my family and [me].

Also, a very kind teenager told [us] our parking lights were on.

Now Papa can go to France with peace of mind I'm in remission.

I really wanted God to show He's really there, and He did. I'll never forget this day. I love you, God!

I'd never seen Lola so happy either.

September 7, 1988

Dear Diary,

Today was my first day of school. I'm in seventh grade at Sayreville Middle School. I saw all my friends and met a couple of new girls. It was super. I'm going to love this year. The only thing I didn't like was [that] I wasn't on the teacher's list 'cause I got [my] schedule changed.

CHAPTER 23

Selected Poems and Last Writings

FOLLOWING ARE SOME of Melissa's touching poems and inspirational last writings:

Life Happiness

The many joys you've spent in eighteen years,
And sometimes you carried with you painful
tears.
But together, day by day,
You've succeeded wonderfully all the way,
And all in time,

*The both of you have been treasured by this
love of mine.*

*Love forever,
Melissa*

Note: This poem was dedicated to us on the occasion of our eighteenth wedding anniversary and was a surprise gift. Melissa gave it to us while we were at Lourdes, France.

Lord's Love

*The Lord's love is my shield.
My faith in Him leads the way.
My pain
Is His pain.
Our love makes us stronger.
My path is to follow the Lord.
My journey ends when He is standing before
my tired eyes.
My destiny is to walk hand in hand with
Him forever.*

The Victory

*The many moments of joy,
And maybe at times some tears.
We've shared these varied feelings
For twelve wonderful years.*

Then when I look back at what I accomplished,
I'm so proud to see
That I accomplished life to the fullest,
Which is to bring my dreams along to the
victory
In the gift of the time that God gave to me.

Four Cherished Gifts

First you gave me life,
Then you gave me love.
Then came beauty.
Lastly came your support,
Even through my mistakes.
These are the most cherished gifts you gave
to me.
They shall never leave my whole heart, soul,
or body.
You were always there when I needed a
helping hand or
When I fell down with disappointment or
was hurt.
You were there to pick me up,
To put me back in my place,
And to start all over again.
When I suffered in misery,
You came to suffer with me,

And you made my suffering come out
with joy.
You were never selfish;
You always shared.
But most of all,
This all means, you see,
You're a special mom who cares.

True Love

If you love someone so much,
You will let them go,
Because in the end you'll know
The pain you go through
Will be for that special being.
You won't let them suffer
In life's miseries.
Love is something you will give,
And at times it may give you
Pain, sadness, or hurt in return,
But you'll see that "being" comes out
In health by your "love".

Thoughts through an Hourglass

Summer darkness.
A slight warm breeze on your face.
Rippling sounds from swaying ocean
currents.

*Your body lingering with all the comforting
beauties.
Soft sands caressing your flesh.
Tiny braces of brightness peeking behind
fragile mists.
Your thoughts flowing like sand through
an hourglass.*

The following poem was composed by Melissa's teachers from Sayreville Middle School and was given to us in a beautiful album signed by 257 classmates and students, along with 26 teachers, upon their learning of Melissa's death on October 9, 1988, at the age of 12.

*When you're feeling sad,
Make a withdrawal from your memory bank,
And soon you will be filled
With the richness of your memories.
And you will slowly smile,
Knowing that
Melissa
Will always be a part of you.*
Sayreville Middle School

Puzzle Piece

*One day about five years ago, I was
diagnosed with ALL, acute lymphocytic
leukemia. I was seven at the time, very
confused about what was going on and
why I was in a hospital with many sick*

people. I thought to myself, I do not belong here.

The biggest part of this devastating tragedy was the battle itself. The chemotherapy made me sick and [caused me to] lose my hair twice, along with the radiation, and my legs got so weak that I couldn't walk for a couple of weeks. But [with] every visit to the clinic, I learned more and more about my illness and what to expect from the chemotherapy. It became part of my everyday life.

The best part of everything was [that] I got a lot of support and love, not only from my family but also from the doctors and nurses who worked with me. They put forth that extra effort just to make sure I was comfortable.

Then in November of 1985, two and half years later, I was finally done with my treatment. I was a free and normal nine-year-old again. I had never before been so happy in my life.

January 13, 1986, came, and the doctor came back with my blood results. They had found blasts. I was so disappointed and angry. It just wasn't fair. All the other nine-year-old children don't have to go through this. I had to start all over again. So I picked up all the pieces and tried to put everything back in its rightful place. Every step of the way, my family stuck by me. We got closer and closer.

Then on August 24, 1987, I had my second relapse. It was a great setback for my family and me, especially since most of our relatives did not live near us. The closest ones were in Jersey City. I lived in the suburbs of Parlin. It is so hard to live a normal life when you don't know what to expect. But from the beginning the doctors really couldn't guarantee anything.

I started treatment again, but this time the treatments were more aggressive. There was no limit to how low my blood count would go. It knocked me out from the beginning.

On January 13, 1988, I had my third relapse. I was eleven years old. This time was much more threatening news than the ones in the past. The doctor said that I would just keep on relapsing and that they didn't know how long I would live. After hearing this, I took a good, long cry to let all the anger and pain out. Then I thought of how my family was going to handle this. It was the worst of all times. My mom [had] just had my baby brother, and [we had] no one to help us.

I lost all hope and wanted to give up. All my dreams had shattered right before my eyes. It was like watching a skyscraper you'd just built fall to the ground [because of] an earthquake. But I didn't give in because I remembered Michelle, Justin, Laela, Jose, and Mary Luz. They were children who were in a difficult battle like [the one] I'm in; [it's] just [that their battles] ended before [the] victory. But they still won because somewhere they are living a new and happy life. I just wanted to take their hopes and dreams with me to the true victory. So I took each day as it came.

On August 24, 1988, I had my fourth relapse. I wasn't really shocked. It became just ordinary news. I did cry a little, but I just kept thinking of how far I wanted to carry on.

Now that I'm twelve years old and I understand what to expect in life, I decided to try again. I knew it wasn't going to be easy, but nobody said it would be. I carry new goals of hope along with me and treasure every moment of my precious gift of life.

Seventeen Happy Years Together

Dear Mommy and Papa,
I thank you so much, with all my heart and soul, for being such terrific parents to me. You gave me all that I needed, [all that I] wanted, and more. It's both of you who joined together and gave me life. I will always love both of you for that, even though at times I don't show it.

You gave me support through my hardest times. Now I think I'm old enough to show you and help you through your hardest time because you're the only parents I want.

Let me see seventeen more happy years together. Happy, happy seventeenth anniversary!
Love always,
Melissa

Inner Thoughts

Yesterday when I was on my way from the hospital, I took a [look] back over my life. For example, [I thought about what] our lives were like before I got sick. Mommy was going to work. I was going to school regularly and then to the babysitter. We would do family outings on the weekends.

Then when I got sick, [we had both] hardships [and] happy moments. [We met] many people [who] helped us and supported us. I was looking for the true meaning of life. To my surprise, I realized that after my trip to France, I have completed my purpose in life or on earth. I don't know what it is about France that [made me feel] I had to go, but it gives me my feeling of fulfillment, the completeness I've been looking for.

I'm not afraid to leave this earth and unite with God because I have my completeness. Some people can live to be one hundred years old and still be looking for their fulfillment, whereas some people can live to be six years and find their fulfillment.

No one else on this earth can feel the great fulfillment that I feel until they have looked back at their lives [to see] if *there is anything missing, and if there is something missing, to do it.*

But the secret is—well, what has worked for me—[that] no matter how many times your hopes, dreams, and goals are shattered, you must pick up the pieces and put them together again. No matter how hard [it is or] how much pain it gives you, in the end you will find your fulfillment.

CHAPTER 24

Melissa's Promise

MELISSA HAD SAID to us on the night before she passed away that whenever she got the chance, she would come and visit us. Others may have some reservations about this, but deep in my heart I truly believe that Melissa has kept her promise.

The initial visit, I believe, took place in the spring of 1989, the first year Melissa was not with us. It was actually on the birthday of my mother, who had passed away several years back in December of 1982. Sylvia and I were busy doing some gardening work in our backyard. After a couple of hours working outside, Sylvia went inside the house through the garage to get a glass of water.

Just as soon as she opened the door, she was overwhelmed by the very nice smell of roses, as if there were a huge garden full of roses. She loudly called me to come over, and I, too, was overpowered by the nice smell of roses, which was quite unbelievable.

We both found ourselves crying as, at that moment, the thought of Melissa completely filled our minds. Later that night, Sylvia and I were discussing what had transpired that morning. I suggested to her that the smell of roses perhaps signified Melissa's first spiritual visit in the company of my mother on the occasion of my mother's birthday.

The second spiritual visit, I believe, occurred on the occasion of Mother's Day, also in the spring of 1989. That was the first year Melissa was not with us to celebrate such a special event. When she was still with us, every Mother's Day she would always have a little gift and a special homemade card for her mom.

As part of our regular activity, after each Sunday mass we would go to the cemetery to light a candle at Melissa's grave. On that particular Sunday, which was also Mother's Day, while at the cemetery praying, Sylvia seemed to be overwhelmed with emotion. She started to cry. Suddenly, a white and brown butterfly, similar to a monarch, flew onto Sylvia's chest and stayed there for a while.

I could see her tears flowing down her cheeks and down to where the butterfly was. To my surprise, the butterfly did not move even though its wings were getting wet with tears. It was only when Sylvia made a motion to wipe her tears that the butterfly flew away.

I firmly believe that those two very unusual occurrences had something to do with Melissa's promise. I also believe they are true manifestations of her undying love for us.

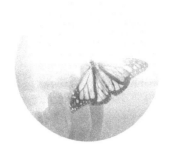

CHAPTER 25

Life without Melissa

DURING THE ENSUING weeks and months after Melissa's death, we naturally went through the difficult phases of grieving. We busied ourselves by trying to reorganize our thoughts and feelings in an effort to gradually resume our prior activities and responsibilities.

Sylvia stayed home and took care of our Bobby. She went back to work once Bobby turned eight years old, working as the accounting manager for a local car dealership located just a few blocks away from Bobby's school. Meanwhile, Bernadette went back to finish high school and subsequently finished college at Rutgers University.

I also went back to work, for the same nonprofit banking trade organization in New York City. I worked there for the next twenty years. About two years after Melissa had passed away, I was promoted to the comptroller position.

During the first quarter of 2007, my company merged with a larger banking trade organization, and I was provided with an early retirement package. However, in June of 2007, at the age of sixty-two, I was offered the position of vice president and CFO at a federal credit union based in northern New Jersey. I accepted the job, retiring in 2011.

Sylvia and I have been retired for almost nine years now and have settled comfortably in an adult community in Monmouth County, New Jersey. We also celebrated our fiftieth wedding anniversary in September of 2020.

Bernadette got married and resides in San Diego with her husband, Rob, and three children: Christian, Taylor, and Ann-Mae. She works in the clinical research industry. Bobby has since graduated from the University of Connecticut's School of Engineering and obtained his master's degree in business from Drexel University. He is currently in project management.

With our guardian angel Melissa watching over us, and with the merciful guidance of the Almighty God, Sylvia and I, despite the hardships and sacrifices we went through, are indeed proud of what we've accomplished so far and are very grateful for God's many blessings.

I have come a long way from a boy who grew up in a poor rural area in the Philippines and who went to grade school without shoes, to presently owning a couple of real estate properties with Sylvia. Being able to send our children to college without having to take out student loans is another accomplishment we are proud of. We are also immensely grateful to have been blessed with very responsible, kind, and caring children and grandchildren.

In continuing my journey through life, I draw upon my father's last word of advice prior to my immigrating to America: "Son, wherever you go and whatever you do, please remember that the true measure of a man's success is not how much wealth, power, or material things he has accumulated over his lifetime. It is measured by how many good deeds he has done for his fellow men."

As we have now reached the golden years of our lives, Sylvia and I have set goals not only to maintain good health and good family relationships but also, and more importantly, to do the things that are pleasing in the eyes of God with the hope that someday perhaps we might be worthy of reuniting with our Melissa.

As we all know, we are definitely passing through on this earth but once. It is therefore imperative that we demonstrate random acts of kindness whenever and wherever the opportunity to do so exists. We must remember that doing good deeds, especially to the least of our brothers and sisters, will never go unnoticed by our Great Creator.

Material things are temporary, but the eternal salvation of the soul is permanent. Trust therefore in the Lord with all your heart and lean not on your own understanding. We must remember that no eyes have seen, nor ears heard, what God has prepared for those who love Him.

It comforts my soul to have witnessed how Melissa embodied such strong faith in our Savior and now rests eternally with Him.

ABOUT THE AUTHOR

Rodrigo T. Gabriel is a devoted husband, father, and man of strong faith. Born in the province of Bulacan, Philippines, he married Sylvia Tiña in 1970, and they immigrated to the United States of America in 1972. He is an accomplished financial executive and lives in Manalapan, New Jersey.